Research Methodology and Basic Biostatistics

For Life Science Students & Researchers

Chelmala Srinivasulu

Made with ♥ on the Notion Press Platform

www.notionpress.com

To my students and research scholars…

Contents

Preface

The genesis of this book lies in my experiences as a professor teaching Research Methodology and supervising doctoral candidates in their research pursuits. Over the years, a pattern emerged that became increasingly apparent: students and scholars who possessed a solid foundation in research methodology and biostatistics consistently produced higher quality research and navigated their academic journeys more successfully than those who struggled with these fundamental concepts.

During my tenure teaching Research Methodology courses, I observed that many students, despite their exceptional subject knowledge, often grappled with the basic principles of research design, methodology, and statistical analysis. This challenge wasn't limited to novice researchers; even experienced scholars sometimes struggled with the conceptual framework necessary for robust research design and execution. This observation led me to recognize a critical gap in the existing educational resources – the need for a comprehensive yet accessible guide to research methodology and biostatistics specifically tailored for life sciences students and researchers.

This book emerged from countless classroom discussions, one-on-one mentoring sessions with research scholars, and the persistent questions that surfaced during research supervision. I noticed that while numerous excellent texts existed on research methodology and statistics, many were either too theoretical to be practically applicable or too complex for beginners to grasp effectively. The need for a bridge between theoretical understanding and practical application became increasingly evident.

The purpose of this book is threefold. First, it aims to demystify the complex concepts of research methodology and biostatistics, presenting them in a clear, logical, and accessible manner. Second, it seeks to provide practical guidance for implementing these concepts in real-world research scenarios. Third, it strives to instill in readers the critical thinking skills necessary for conducting meaningful research in the life sciences.

In writing this book, I have drawn not only from my academic experience but also from the real challenges and questions posed by my students and research scholars. Each chapter has been carefully structured to build understanding progressively, incorporating examples from actual research scenarios and addressing common misconceptions that I've encountered in my teaching career.

The journey of writing this book has been both challenging and rewarding. It required distilling years of teaching experience and research supervision into a coherent narrative that would serve both novice researchers and experienced scholars. The process involved countless revisions and refinements, each aimed at making complex concepts more accessible without sacrificing scientific rigor.

A unique feature of this book is its integrated approach to research methodology and biostatistics. Rather than treating these as separate entities, the text weaves them together to demonstrate their interdependence in modern research. This integration reflects the reality of contemporary research practices, where methodological choices and statistical analyses are inextricably linked.

I am deeply grateful to my students and research scholars whose questions, challenges, and insights have contributed immensely to shaping this book. Their diverse perspectives and needs have helped ensure that the content remains relevant and practical. Special thanks are also due to my colleagues who provided valuable feedback and suggestions during the writing process.

It is my sincere hope that this book will serve as a valuable resource for students and researchers in the life sciences, helping them develop the methodological and statistical foundations necessary for conducting meaningful research. As research continues to evolve with new technologies and approaches, the fundamental principles outlined in this book remain essential for ensuring scientific rigor and validity in research endeavors.

Whether you are a student beginning your research journey, a scholar advancing your academic career, or a professional researcher seeking to refresh your methodological knowledge, I trust this book will provide the guidance and clarity you seek in your pursuit of scientific excellence.

Chelmala Srinivasulu
Professor
Osmania University

Acknowledgments

The creation of this book has been a journey enriched by the contributions, support, and interactions of many individuals to whom I am deeply grateful.

First and foremost, I extend my heartfelt gratitude to my students and research scholars whose inquisitive minds and persistent questions have been the driving force behind this book. Their varied perspectives, honest expressions of anxiety, and genuine desire to understand research methodology have helped shape this work into something truly practical and meaningful. Their challenges became my inspiration, and their progress, my reward.

I am particularly indebted to my academic colleagues and peers who generously shared their expertise and experiences. Their insightful suggestions, constructive criticisms, and scholarly discussions have significantly enhanced the depth and breadth of this book. The collaborative spirit of academia has never been more evident than in their willingness to engage in lengthy discussions about research methodology and statistical applications.

Special appreciation goes to Dr Bhargavi, my wife and partner in research, who provided valuable feedback on early drafts and shared her own experiences in teaching research methodology. My deepest gratitude to her for her unwavering support and sharp critical eye have been invaluable throughout this writing process. Her ability to provide both constructive criticism and encouragement at exactly the right moments has been crucial to the completion of this work. Her patience during the long hours of writing and revision, combined with her insights as a first reader, have significantly enhanced the clarity and accessibility of this text.

Finally, I thank all those unnamed individuals - students, researchers, and colleagues - whose questions, comments, and discussions over the years have contributed to my understanding of how to better teach and explain research methodology and biostatistics. Their collective influence permeates every page of this book.

To all of you, my sincere thanks.

Chelmala Srinivasulu

Introduction

Somewhere, something incredible is waiting to be known.

- *Carl Sagan*

Research methodology and biostatistics form the cornerstone of scientific inquiry in the life sciences, providing researchers with the essential tools and frameworks necessary for conducting rigorous, meaningful, and ethically sound investigations. As the complexity of biological systems and the sophistication of research techniques continue to advance, a solid foundation in research methodology and statistical analysis becomes increasingly crucial for students and researchers alike.

This comprehensive guide serves as an essential resource for understanding the fundamental principles and practical applications of research methodology in the life sciences. From the conceptualization of research questions to the analysis and presentation of findings, this book provides a structured approach to scientific investigation that balances theoretical understanding with practical implementation. The integration of biostatistical concepts throughout the text reflects the inseparable nature of research design and data analysis in modern scientific inquiry.

For students entering the field of life sciences, this book offers a systematic introduction to the research process, helping them develop the critical thinking skills necessary for scientific investigation. It bridges the gap between theoretical knowledge and practical application, providing clear guidelines for designing studies, collecting data, and interpreting results. The incorporation of real-world examples and case studies helps illustrate the practical implications of methodological choices and statistical approaches.

Experienced researchers will find this book valuable as a comprehensive reference that covers both traditional and emerging research methodologies. The detailed discussion of experimental design, sampling techniques, and statistical analysis provides the tools necessary for planning and executing research projects that meet the highest standards of scientific rigor. Special attention is given to the ethical considerations that must guide all research involving living systems, ensuring that scientific advancement proceeds with appropriate respect for both human and animal subjects.

The inclusion of biostatistics as a central component of this text reflects its critical role in modern research. From understanding the basics of biostatistics to complex analyses, explained in a simple manner, researchers must be able to select and apply appropriate statistical methods to draw valid conclusions from their data. This book provides clear explanations of statistical concepts and their applications, making complex analytical techniques accessible to readers at all levels of statistical expertise.

In an era of rapid technological advancement and increasing data complexity, the principles outlined in this book become even more relevant. The proliferation of high-throughput technologies and big data approaches in life sciences research demands a solid understanding of both traditional and emerging methodological approaches. This book addresses these contemporary challenges while maintaining focus on the fundamental principles that underpin all scientific investigation.

The structure of this book progressively builds understanding, beginning with basic concepts and moving toward more complex methodological and statistical applications. Special attention is given to common challenges and pitfalls in research design and analysis, providing readers with strategies to identify and address potential problems before they impact research outcomes.

Chapter 1 Introduction to Research Methodology provides the foundational understanding of research in life sciences. It explores the systematic nature of research, different types of research (basic, applied, descriptive, exploratory, etc.), and key concepts including variables, hypotheses, and constructs. The chapter emphasizes how systematic investigation has transformed our understanding of life sciences, from molecular biology to ecosystem dynamics, while establishing the importance of methodological frameworks in scientific inquiry.

Chapter 2 Research Process and Study Design outlines the systematic approach to conducting research, from initial problem formulation to study completion. It details the eight-step research model, covering problem formulation, literature review, research design selection, data collection planning, implementation, analysis, interpretation, and reporting. Special attention is given to the identification of research gaps, conceptual framework development, and various study design options including experimental, quasi-experimental, and observational approaches.

Chapter 3 Data Collection Techniques examines various methods of gathering research data in life sciences. It covers both primary data collection methods (surveys, interviews, observations, experimental methods) and secondary data collection approaches. The chapter discusses the distinctions between qualitative and quantitative data collection, mixed methods approaches, and the importance of ethical considerations in data gathering. Practical strategies for maintaining data quality and integrity are also addressed.

Chapter 4 Measurement and Scaling Techniques focuses on the principles and practices of scientific measurement. It explores different types of measurement scales (nominal, ordinal, interval, ratio), techniques for ensuring measurement reliability and validity, and strategies for improving measurement quality. The chapter emphasizes the importance of precise measurement in life sciences research and provides practical guidelines for maintaining measurement accuracy.

Chapter 5 Biostatistical Foundations introduces essential statistical concepts for life sciences research. It covers descriptive statistics, probability distributions, and the basics of inferential statistics. The chapter discusses various statistical software tools and their applications, while emphasizing the importance of appropriate statistical analysis in research design and interpretation.

Chapter 6 Hypothesis Testing provides a comprehensive overview of hypothesis testing in scientific research. It covers the formulation of hypotheses, steps in hypothesis testing, understanding p-values and significance levels, and common statistical tests. The chapter emphasizes the importance of proper test selection and interpretation of results while acknowledging potential errors in hypothesis testing.

Chapter 7 Ethical Considerations in Research addresses the crucial ethical aspects of conducting research in life sciences. It covers ethics in human participant research, animal studies, principles of informed consent, and the role of institutional review boards. The chapter emphasizes the importance of maintaining research integrity while addressing issues of research misconduct and bias.

Chapter 8 Writing and Communicating Research Findings focuses on effectively communicating research results to various audiences. It provides guidance on structuring research reports, conducting literature reviews, interpreting and discussing results, and presenting data visually. The chapter also covers practical aspects of publishing research, including journal submission processes and conference presentations.

Each chapter builds upon the previous ones, creating a comprehensive understanding of research methodology and biostatistics in life sciences. The text emphasizes practical application while maintaining theoretical rigor, making it valuable for both students and experienced researchers in the field. As we advance into an era of increasingly collaborative and interdisciplinary research, the ability to understand and apply proper research methodology becomes essential for effective communication across scientific disciplines. This book provides the common language and conceptual framework necessary for such collaboration, while maintaining specific focus on applications in the life sciences.

Through mastery of the concepts presented in this text, readers will develop the skills necessary to design, conduct, and analyze research that contributes meaningfully to scientific knowledge. Whether pursuing academic research, clinical trials, or applied scientific investigation, the principles and practices outlined here provide the foundation for rigorous and meaningful scientific inquiry in the life sciences.

1. Introduction to Research Methodology

Research is formalized curiosity. It is poking and prying with a purpose.

-   Zora Neale Hurston

Research methodology forms the backbone of scientific inquiry in the life sciences, serving as the foundational framework through which we advance our understanding of the living world. As we embark on this exploration of research methodology, we'll discover how systematic investigation has transformed our understanding of life itself, from the molecular intricacies of DNA to the complex dynamics of entire ecosystems.

1.1 Overview of Research in Life Sciences

Research, in its most fundamental form, represents humanity's systematic pursuit of knowledge. Unlike casual observation or random discovery, research embodies a structured, methodical approach to understanding phenomena. In the life sciences, this systematic investigation takes on particular significance as it deals with the complexity of living systems, their interactions, and their impact on human health and the environment.

To truly understand research in life sciences, we must first grasp its essential nature. Research can be defined as a systematic and methodical process of inquiry that aims to discover, interpret, or revise facts, theories, or practical applications. However, this definition only scratches the surface of what research truly encompasses. Let's delve deeper into its characteristics and implications.

The systematic nature of research sets it apart from other forms of investigation. When scientists conduct research, they follow a carefully planned sequence of steps, each building upon the previous one. This methodical approach ensures that findings are reliable, replicable, and contribute meaningfully to the existing body of knowledge. Consider, for example, the discovery of penicillin by Alexander Fleming in 1928. While the initial observation of bacterial inhibition around a mold colony might have been serendipitous, it was Fleming's systematic investigation that transformed this observation into a groundbreaking scientific discovery.

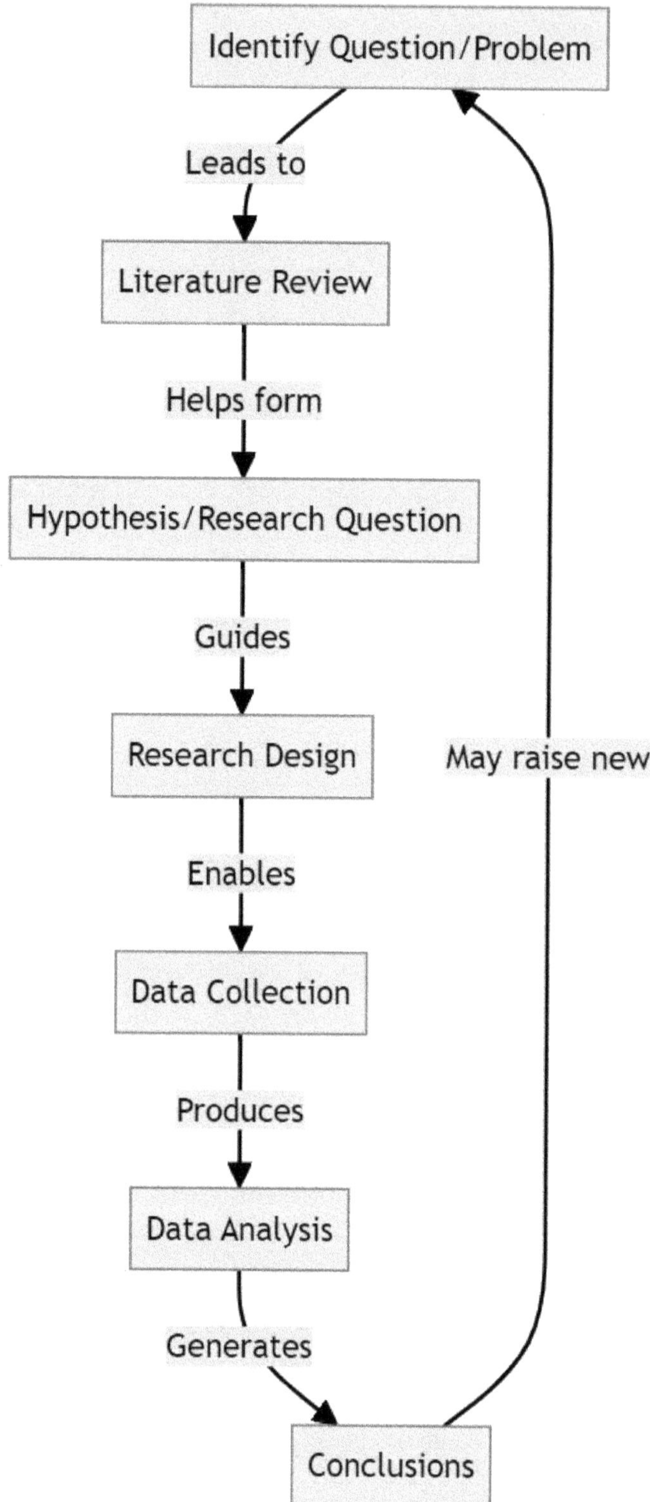

Fig. 1.1. Detailed Research Process Flow

The scope of research in life sciences is remarkably broad, encompassing everything from molecular biology to ecosystem dynamics. At the molecular level, researchers probe the fundamental mechanisms of life itself. They investigate how genes are expressed, how proteins interact, and how cells communicate with one another. This microscopic realm of research has led to revolutionary breakthroughs in our understanding of diseases, development, and the basic processes that sustain life.

Moving up the organizational hierarchy, organismal research examines how individual organisms function, develop, and behave. This level of investigation has provided crucial insights into human health, animal behavior, and plant biology. For instance, studies of model organisms like *Drosophila melanogaster* (fruit fly) have revealed fundamental principles of genetics and development that apply across species.

Population-level research broadens the scope further, examining how groups of organisms interact, evolve, and adapt over time. This includes epidemiological studies that track disease patterns in human populations, conservation biology research that monitors endangered species, and evolutionary studies that investigate how species change over generations.

Environmental research in the life sciences addresses the complex relationships between organisms and their surroundings. This field has become increasingly crucial as we face global challenges like climate change, habitat destruction, and biodiversity loss. Research at this level often requires integration of multiple disciplines, from molecular biology to ecology, highlighting the interconnected nature of biological systems.

The importance of research in advancing life sciences cannot be overstated. Every major breakthrough in medicine, biotechnology, and our understanding of life has its roots in careful research. The development of vaccines, the mapping of the human genome, and our growing understanding of neurodegenerative diseases all stem from systematic research efforts.

1.2 Purposes and Applications of Research

The pursuit of research in life sciences serves dual purposes: the advancement of fundamental knowledge and its practical application in solving real-world problems. This duality creates a dynamic relationship between pure scientific understanding and its practical implementation, forming a continuum rather than a strict dichotomy.

Knowledge advancement, often termed pure or basic research, represents humanity's quest to understand the fundamental nature of life and its processes. This type of research might appear abstract or disconnected from immediate practical concerns, yet it forms the essential foundation upon which applied research builds. Consider the discovery of DNA's structure by Watson and Crick in 1953. While this breakthrough initially appeared to be purely theoretical, it eventually revolutionized fields ranging from medicine to forensic science, demonstrating how fundamental research can lead to unexpected practical applications.

The process of knowledge advancement in life sciences often follows unexpected paths. Researchers studying the basic biology of bacteria in extreme environments, for instance, discovered heat-stable enzymes that would later become crucial tools in molecular biology and diagnostic testing. This example illustrates how pure research, driven by curiosity rather than immediate practical goals, can yield profound practical benefits that were impossible to predict at the outset.

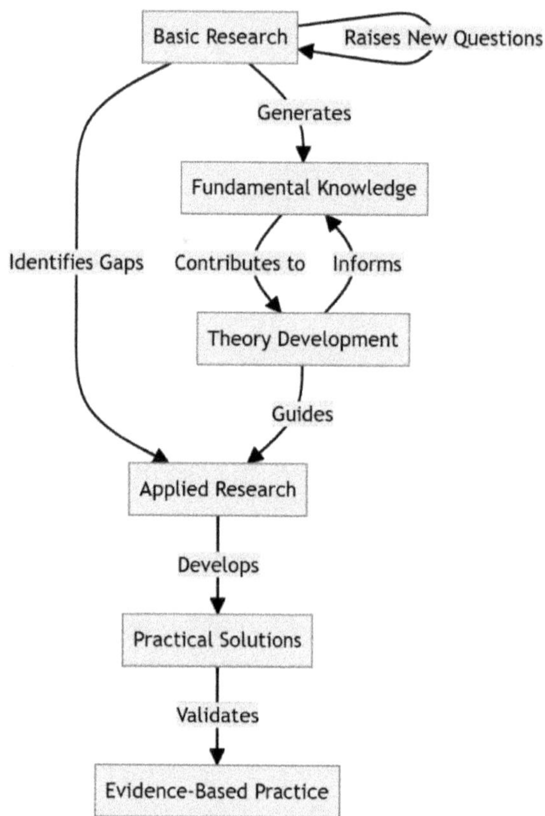

Fig. 1.2. Knowledge to Application Pipeline

The role of research in evidence-based practice represents one of the most significant applications of scientific investigation in the life sciences. Evidence-based practice integrates the best available research evidence with practical expertise and individual circumstances to make informed decisions. This approach has transformed numerous fields, particularly medicine and healthcare, where treatment decisions now rely heavily on scientific evidence rather than tradition or individual experience alone.

Consider the development of modern cancer treatments. The journey from laboratory discovery to clinical application illustrates the complex interplay between different types of research. Basic research into cell division mechanisms led to the understanding of how cancer cells proliferate. This knowledge informed applied research into potential drug targets, eventually resulting in the development of targeted therapies. Clinical trials then evaluated these treatments' effectiveness, generating evidence that now guides medical practice. This progression demonstrates how different forms of research contribute to solving real-world problems.

The practical applications of research extend far beyond medicine. In agriculture, research has led to improved crop yields, pest resistance, and sustainable farming practices. Environmental research guides conservation efforts and policy decisions about resource management. Biotechnology research has spawned entire industries, from pharmaceutical development to biofuel production.

Modern research increasingly emphasizes translational approaches, which aim to bridge the gap between basic scientific discoveries and their practical applications. This "bench-to-bedside" approach in medical research, for instance, accelerates the process of turning laboratory discoveries into effective treatments. Similar translational approaches exist in other areas of life sciences, such as converting basic ecological research into effective conservation strategies.

The application of research findings requires careful consideration of context and limitations. What works in a laboratory setting may face unexpected challenges in real-world applications. This reality has led to the development of implementation science, which studies how to effectively translate research findings into practice while accounting for real-world constraints and variations.

Evidence-based practice has evolved to include multiple levels of evidence, arranged in a hierarchy that helps practitioners evaluate the strength of research support for different approaches. This hierarchy typically places systematic reviews and meta-analyses at the top, followed by randomized controlled trials, cohort studies, case-control studies, and expert opinions. Understanding this hierarchy helps practitioners make informed decisions while recognizing the varying degrees of certainty associated with different types of evidence.

1.3 Types of Research

The diverse nature of scientific inquiry in life sciences has given rise to various research types, each serving distinct purposes and employing different methodological approaches. Understanding these different types of research is crucial for selecting appropriate methods to address specific research questions and for critically evaluating published research findings.

The fundamental distinction between basic and applied research represents more than just a simple categorization; it reflects different philosophical approaches to scientific inquiry. Basic research, often called pure or fundamental research, seeks to expand human knowledge without immediate practical applications in mind. This type of research asks questions about fundamental biological processes, natural phenomena, and theoretical relationships.

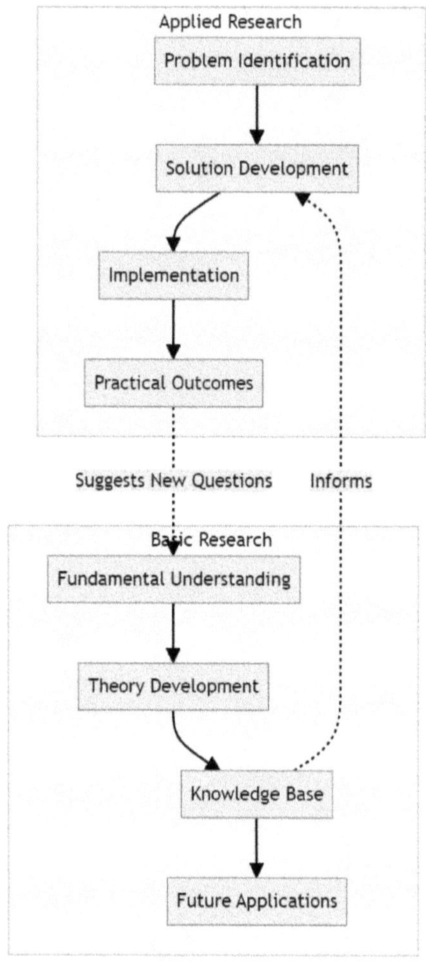

Fig. 1.3. Basic vs Applied Research Comparison

1.3.1 Descriptive research

Descriptive research plays a crucial role in life sciences by providing detailed accounts of biological phenomena. This type of research answers the "what," "where," and "when" questions that form the foundation for more complex investigations. For example, early naturalists' descriptive studies of species distribution and characteristics laid the groundwork for Darwin's theory of evolution. Modern descriptive research continues this tradition using sophisticated tools and methods, from electron microscopy to satellite tracking of animal migrations.

The value of descriptive research lies in its ability to provide comprehensive documentation of phenomena in their natural state. When researchers first encountered COVID-19, descriptive studies of symptoms, transmission patterns, and disease progression were crucial for understanding the novel virus. These studies provided the foundation for subsequent explanatory and experimental research into treatments and vaccines.

Comprehensive Research Types Analysis					
Research Type	**Primary Goal**	**Methodology Characteristics**	**Example in Life Sciences**	**Strengths**	**Limitations**
Basic Research	Fundamental understanding	• Controlled conditions • Rigorous experimental design • Theory-focused	Study of DNA repair mechanisms	• Builds theoretical framework • Discovers new principles • High internal validity	• May lack immediate application • Often requires significant resources • May be difficult to translate
Applied Research	Practical solutions	• Real-world settings • Problem-focused • Implementation-oriented	Development of new antibiotics	• Direct practical impact • Clear objectives • Immediate relevance	• May oversimplify complex phenomena • Context-dependent results • Time pressure constraints
Descriptive Research	Detailed characterization	• Observational methods • Natural settings • Comprehensive documentation	Mapping biodiversity in a region	• Rich, detailed data • Natural conditions • Multiple variables considered	• No causal conclusions • Potential observer bias • Time-intensive
Exploratory Research	Initial understanding	• Flexible design • Multiple approaches • Hypothesis generation	Investigation of novel diseases	• Generates new ideas • Adaptable methods • Opens new research areas	• Limited generalizability • Preliminary findings • May lack precision
Explanatory Research	Causal relationships	• Controlled experiments • Hypothesis testing • Statistical analysis	Drug efficacy studies	• Establishes causation • Quantifiable results • High reliability	• May oversimplify • Artificial conditions • Limited variables
Analytical Research	Critical evaluation	• Systematic review • Meta-analysis • Data synthesis	Treatment effectiveness comparison	• Comprehensive overview • Evidence synthesis • Identifies patterns	• Dependent on existing data • Publication bias • Time lag

1.3.2 Exploratory research

Exploratory research serves as the scientific equivalent of reconnaissance, venturing into unknown territory to identify potential areas for more detailed investigation. This type of research is particularly valuable when dealing with novel phenomena or when existing theories fail to explain observed patterns. Exploratory research is characterized by its flexibility and openness to unexpected findings.

Consider the field of microbiome research. Initial exploratory studies revealed the unexpected complexity and importance of bacterial communities in human health. These findings opened entirely new research directions, leading to our current understanding of the microbiome's role in everything from digestion to mental health.

1.3.3 Explanatory research

Explanatory research seeks to understand cause-and-effect relationships through carefully controlled studies. This type of research typically follows descriptive and exploratory work, testing specific hypotheses about how and why phenomena occur. The strength of explanatory research lies in its ability to isolate variables and establish causal relationships.

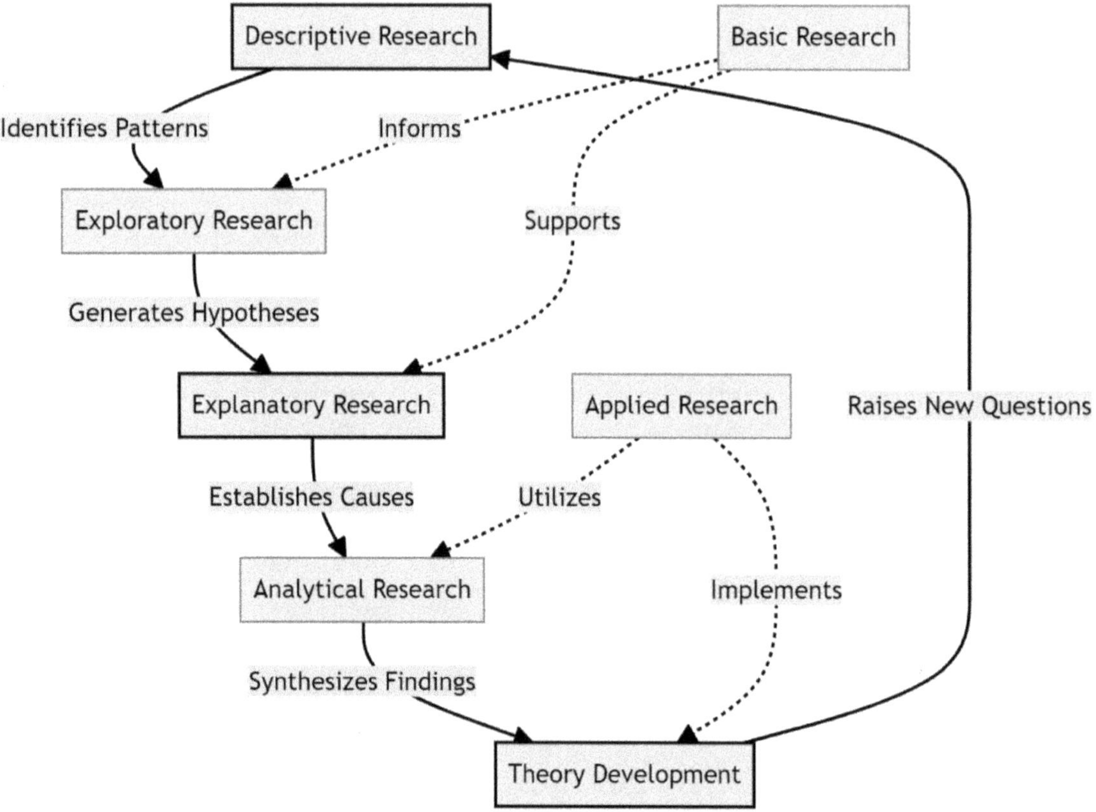

Fig. 1.4. Research Process Development Flow

1.3.4 Analytical research

Analytical research represents a higher level of scientific inquiry, focusing on why phenomena occur and what they mean in a broader context. This type of research often synthesizes findings from multiple studies, identifying patterns and relationships that might not be apparent in individual investigations. Meta-analyses and systematic reviews are common forms of analytical research that have become increasingly important in evidence-based practice.

1.4 Key Concepts in Research Methodology

Understanding the fundamental concepts in research methodology provides the essential framework for conducting meaningful scientific investigations. These concepts serve as the building blocks for research design, data collection, and analysis, ultimately determining the validity and reliability of research findings.

1.4.1 Variables

Variables represent one of the most crucial concepts in research methodology. In the context of life sciences research, variables are characteristics or conditions that can change or vary across different observations. The proper identification, control, and measurement of variables often determine the success of a research project.

Independent variables, often manipulated by researchers, represent the factors hypothesized to cause or influence changes in other variables. For instance, in a study examining the effects of exercise on cardiovascular health, the exercise regimen (type, duration, intensity) would constitute the independent variables. Researchers carefully control these variables to understand their impact on the outcomes of interest.

Dependent variables, on the other hand, represent the outcomes or responses measured in response to changes in independent variables. In our exercise study example, dependent variables might include heart rate, blood pressure, or cholesterol levels. The relationship between independent and dependent variables forms the core of many research hypotheses.

Control variables introduce an additional layer of complexity to research design. These are factors that researchers hold constant to prevent them from influencing the relationship between independent and dependent variables. For example, when studying the effects of a new drug, researchers might control for participants' age, gender, and pre-existing conditions to isolate the drug's specific effects.

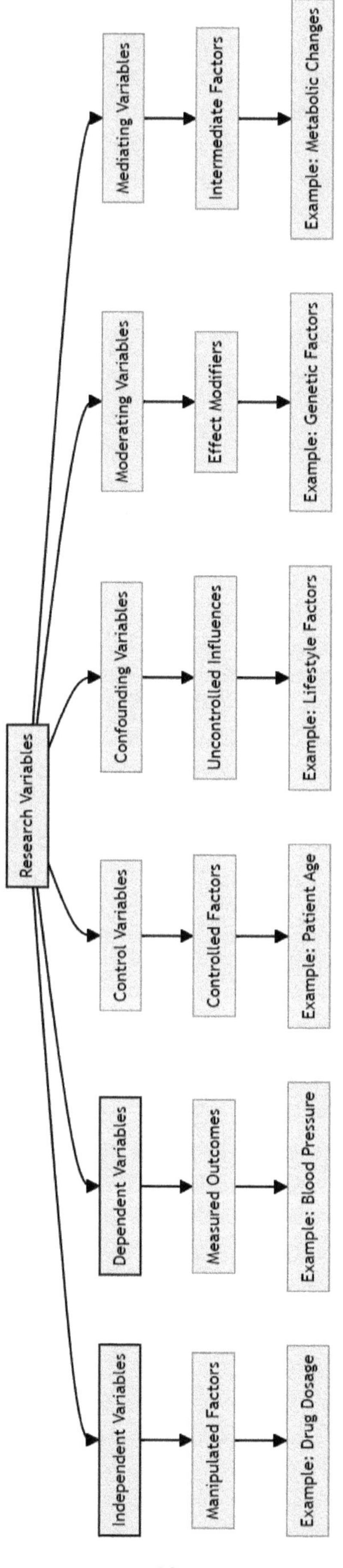

Fig. 1.5. Complex Variable Relationships in Research

Confounding variables pose particular challenges in research methodology. These are unexpected or uncontrolled factors that might influence the relationship between independent and dependent variables, potentially leading to spurious conclusions. Consider a study examining the relationship between coffee consumption and cardiovascular health. Stress levels might act as a confounding variable, as stressed individuals might consume more coffee and also have poorer cardiovascular health independently of their coffee consumption.

The concept of constructs represents another fundamental aspect of research methodology. Constructs are abstract ideas or theoretical concepts that cannot be directly observed but must be inferred through measurable indicators. In life sciences research, many important variables are actually constructs that require careful operationalization.

Construct Operationalization Framework				
Construct	**Definition**	**Operational Indicators**	**Measurement Tools**	**Considerations**
Stress	Physiological and psychological response to demands	• Cortisol levels • Heart rate variability • Self-reported anxiety • Blood pressure	• Blood tests • ECG monitoring • Psychological scales • Sphygmomanometer	• Temporal variations • Individual differences • Environmental factors
Quality of Life	Overall well-being and life satisfaction	• Physical functioning • Mental health • Social relationships • Environmental factors	• SF-36 questionnaire • WHO QOL scale • Functional assessments • Social network analysis	• Cultural differences • Subjective nature • Multiple domains
Immune Function	Ability to resist infection and disease	• White blood cell count • Antibody levels • Inflammatory markers • Recovery time	• Blood analysis • ELISA tests • Clinical observations • Challenge tests	• Circadian rhythms • Age effects • Environmental impacts
Fitness Level	Physical capability and endurance	• VO2 max • Muscle strength • Flexibility • Body composition	• Exercise testing • Dynamometer • Flexibility tests • DEXA scans	• Training status • Gender differences • Testing conditions

1.4.2 The Scientific Method

The scientific method provides the overarching framework within which these concepts operate. This systematic approach to inquiry involves several key steps: observation, question formulation, hypothesis development, experimental design, data collection, analysis, and conclusion drawing. Each step builds upon the previous ones, creating a logical progression from initial curiosity to substantiated findings.

Consider the development of a new therapeutic drug. The process begins with observations about disease mechanisms (constructs) and potential therapeutic targets (variables). Researchers formulate hypotheses about how targeting specific molecular pathways might affect disease outcomes. They design experiments controlling for various factors while measuring both direct effects (dependent variables) and potential side effects (additional variables). Throughout this process, researchers must carefully consider how to operationalize abstract concepts into measurable variables and how to account for potential confounding factors.

The integration of these key concepts – variables, constructs, and hypotheses – within the scientific method framework enables researchers to conduct rigorous investigations while maintaining awareness of potential limitations and sources of error. This understanding is crucial for both conducting research and critically evaluating published findings in the life sciences.

1.4.3 Hypotheses

Hypotheses represent testable predictions about relationships between variables. The formulation of clear, specific hypotheses is crucial for directing research efforts and evaluating outcomes. In life sciences research, hypotheses typically emerge from theoretical frameworks, previous research findings, or observed patterns in preliminary data.

The **null hypothesis (H_0)** states that no relationship exists between the variables under investigation. It serves as a statistical starting point, assuming that any observed differences or relationships occur by chance alone. The **alternative hypothesis (H_1)** proposes the existence of a specific relationship or effect. Together, these hypotheses form the basis for statistical testing and inference.

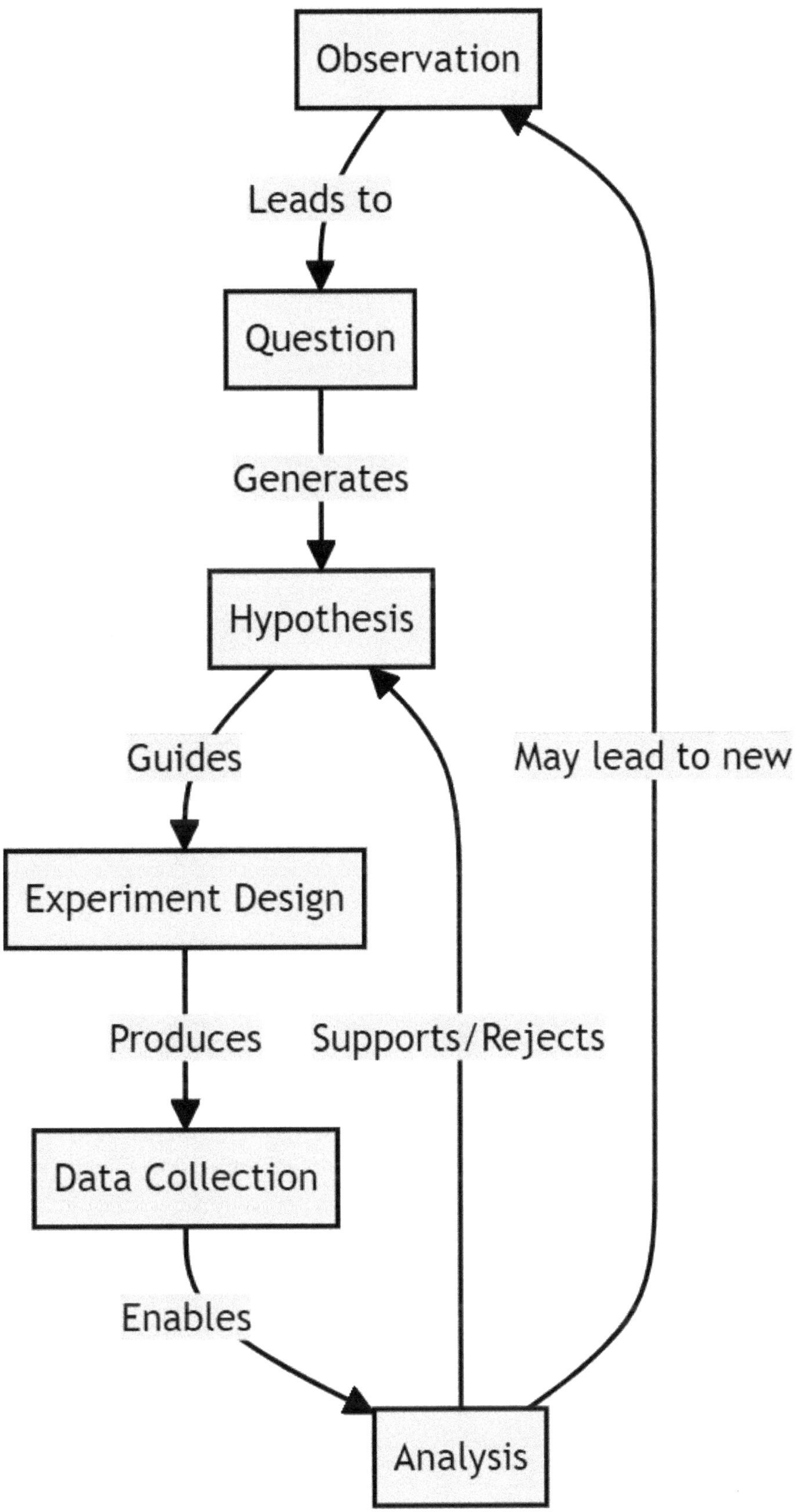

Fig. 1.6. The Scientific Method Process

This page is left blank intentionally.

2. Research Process and Study Design

Research is to see what everybody else has seen, and to think what nobody else has thought.

-   Albert Szent-Györgyi

The journey from initial scientific curiosity to meaningful research findings requires careful planning, systematic execution, and thoughtful design. This chapter explores the structured approach to conducting research in life sciences, providing a comprehensive framework for developing and implementing research studies.

2.1 Overview of the Research Process

The research process represents a systematic journey of scientific inquiry, following a structured yet dynamic path from initial curiosity to conclusive findings. While often presented as a linear sequence, the research process is inherently iterative, with each step informing and potentially modifying previous decisions.

The eight-step research model provides a comprehensive framework for conducting scientific research. Let's examine each step in detail:

Step 1. **Problem Formulation**

The research process begins with identifying and clearly defining the research problem. This crucial first step shapes all subsequent decisions and activities. Consider the case of researchers studying antibiotic resistance. Their initial observation of increasing treatment failures must be transformed into specific, answerable research questions. This step involves careful consideration of the problem's scope, significance, and feasibility of investigation.

Step 2. **Literature Review**

This step involves systematically examining existing knowledge about the research problem. Modern researchers have access to vast databases of scientific literature, requiring sophisticated search and analysis strategies. For instance, in our antibiotic resistance example, researchers would need to review studies on resistance mechanisms, prevalence patterns, and previous intervention attempts.

Step 3. **Research Design**

The design phase translates research questions into concrete plans for investigation. This step requires careful consideration of methodological options, potential limitations, and resource requirements. Researchers studying antibiotic resistance might choose between experimental studies of resistance mechanisms or epidemiological studies of resistance patterns.

Step 4. **Data Collection Planning**

This step involves developing detailed protocols for gathering information. Researchers must consider sampling strategies, measurement tools, and quality control measures. For instance, studying antibiotic resistance might require planning for laboratory protocols, patient sampling procedures, and data recording methods.

Step 5. **Data Collection**

The execution phase where planned procedures are implemented to gather information. This step often requires careful attention to standardization, quality control, and ethical considerations. In our example, this might involve collecting bacterial samples, conducting susceptibility tests, and recording patient data.

Step 6. **Data Analysis**

Raw data must be processed and analyzed to extract meaningful insights. This step involves both statistical analysis and interpretation of patterns. Researchers studying antibiotic resistance would need to analyze resistance patterns, identify risk factors, and evaluate intervention effectiveness.

Step 7. **Interpretation**

Analysis results must be interpreted within the context of existing knowledge and study limitations. This step involves critical thinking and careful consideration of alternative explanations. Researchers must consider how their findings contribute to understanding antibiotic resistance and their practical implications.

Step 8. **Research Reporting**

The final step involves communicating findings to the scientific community and relevant stakeholders. This includes preparing manuscripts for publication, presenting at conferences, and often developing recommendations for practice.

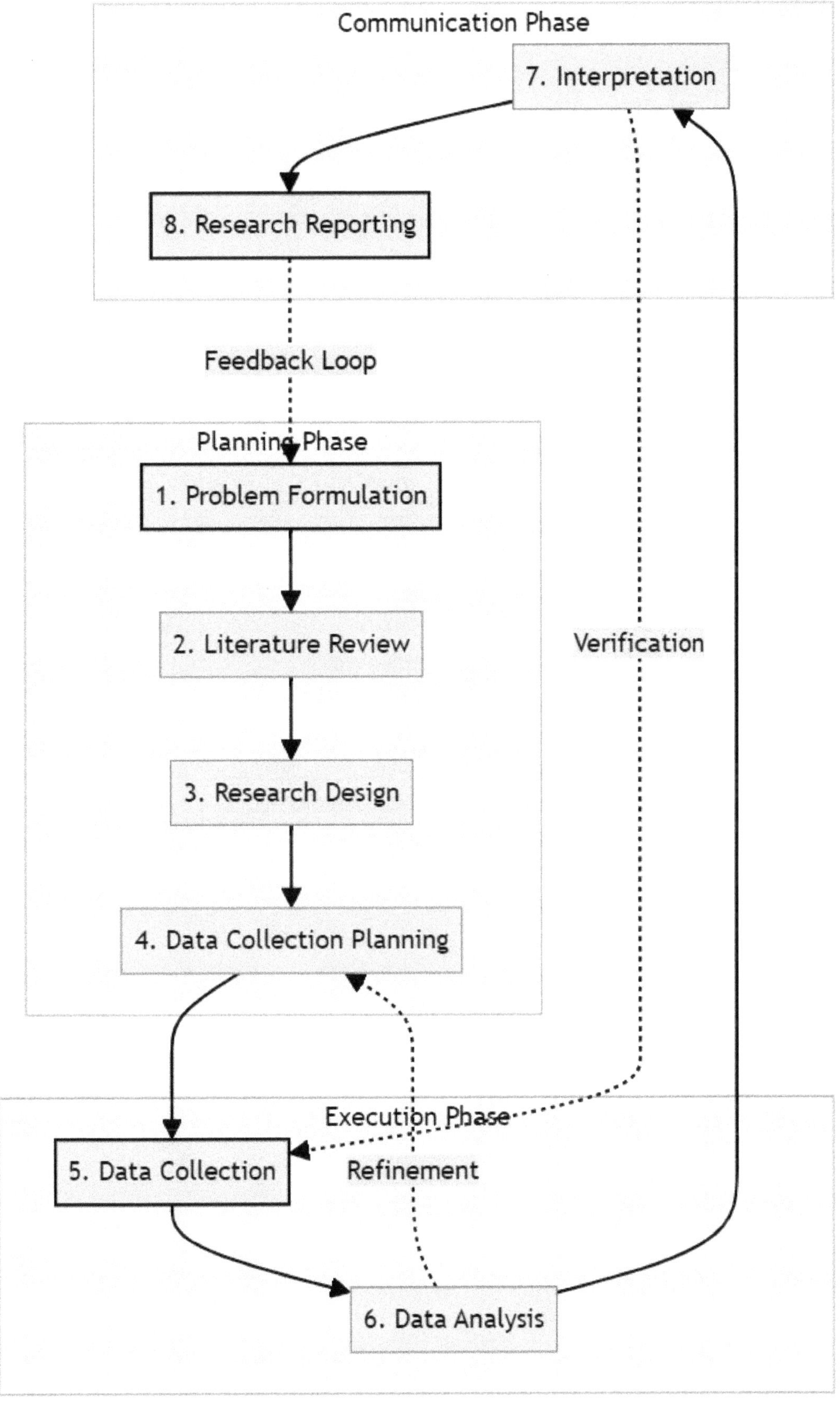

Fig. 2.1. Eight-Step Research Process Model

The cyclic nature of research becomes evident through various feedback loops within this process.

For example:

Research Process Feedback Loops			
Feedback Loop Type	**Description**	**Example**	**Impact**
Data Quality Loop	Real-time monitoring of data quality during collection	Identifying inconsistencies in measurement techniques	Leads to protocol refinements
Analysis Loop	Preliminary results suggesting need for additional data	Discovery of unexpected correlations requiring further investigation	Additional data collection or revised analysis plans
Interpretation Loop	New findings raising questions about initial assumptions	Unexpected resistance mechanisms suggesting new research directions	Modification of research questions or hypotheses
Implementation Loop	Practical application revealing new research needs	Clinical implementation revealing unforeseen challenges	New research projects or study modifications
Literature Loop	New publications affecting ongoing research	Publication of related findings during study execution	Adjustment of research focus or methods

2.2 Formulating a Research Problem

Conducting research is a systematic process of inquiry and investigation, aiming to expand knowledge and understanding within a particular field or domain. At the heart of any research endeavor lies the research problem - the central issue or question that the study seeks to address. Formulating a research problem is a critical step in the research process, as it sets the foundation for the entire study and guides the researcher's subsequent actions.

The research problem is the starting point that initiates the research journey. It is the specific question or set of questions that the researcher wants to explore, investigate, and ultimately answer through their study. Formulating a well-defined research problem is essential for ensuring the relevance, feasibility, and potential contribution of the research.

2.2.1 Steps in Formulating Research Problem

To formulate an effective research problem, researchers typically engage in a thoughtful and iterative process that involves the following key steps:

1. **Identifying the Research Area and Reviewing Existing Literature**: The first step in formulating a research problem is to identify the broad research area or domain of interest. This involves conducting a comprehensive review of the existing literature, such as academic journals, books, and other relevant sources, to gain a deep understanding of the current state of knowledge in the field. This review helps the researcher identify gaps, controversies, or areas that warrant further investigation.

2. **Defining the Research Focus**: Based on the insights gained from the literature review, the researcher can then narrow down the research focus and begin to formulate a more specific research problem. This may involve identifying a specific phenomenon, theory, or issue that the researcher aims to explore in greater depth.

3. **Clarifying the Research Objectives and Questions**: The research problem should be translated into clear and focused research objectives and questions. These objectives and questions should be specific, measurable, and aligned with the overall research goals. They should also be feasible to address within the scope and constraints of the study.

4. **Considering the Significance and Potential Contribution**: A well-formulated research problem should not only address a gap or issue in the existing literature but also have the potential to make a meaningful contribution to the field. The researcher should carefully consider the potential theoretical, practical, or methodological implications of the research and how it can advance knowledge or solve a real-world problem.

5. **Evaluating the Feasibility and Limitations**: Finally, the researcher should assess the feasibility of the research problem in terms of available resources, time, and access to data or participants. It is important to identify any potential limitations or constraints that may impact the study's scope or the ability to draw reliable conclusions.

By following these steps, researchers can develop a clearly articulated research problem that serves as a guide for the entire research process. A well-formulated research problem provides a focused direction for the study, facilitates the selection of appropriate research methods, and ensures that the findings and conclusions are relevant and impactful within the field of study.

Ultimately, the formulation of a research problem is a crucial step in the research process, as it lays the groundwork for a meaningful and productive investigation that can contribute to the advancement of knowledge and understanding.

2.3 Identification of research gaps

Identifying research gaps requires systematic analysis of existing knowledge and current needs in the field. This process involves several key activities:

1. Environmental Scanning

Researchers must stay attuned to developments in their field through:

- Regular review of current literature

- Attendance at scientific conferences

- Engagement with professional networks

- Awareness of practical challenges in the field

2. Gap Analysis

This involves systematic identification of areas where current knowledge is insufficient:

- Contradictions in existing research

- Unexplained phenomena

- Practical problems lacking solutions

- Theoretical inconsistencies

2.4 Literature Review

A literature review is a comprehensive examination and synthesis of the existing scholarly work on a particular topic or research question. It serves as a critical analysis and evaluation of the current state of knowledge in a field of study.

The primary purposes of a literature review are:

- To identify and summarize the key theories, concepts, and empirical findings relevant to the research problem.

- To highlight the gaps, inconsistencies, or contradictions in the existing literature.

- To position the current research within the broader context of the field and demonstrate its significance.

The process of conducting a literature review typically involves the following steps:

Defining the research question or topic: The literature review should be guided by a clear and focused research question or topic that the review aims to address.

Searching and selecting relevant sources: This involves systematically searching for and identifying scholarly articles, books, dissertations, and other relevant materials that are pertinent to the research question.

Critically evaluating the sources: The researcher should carefully analyze and assess the quality, credibility, and relevance of the selected sources, considering factors such as research methods, data analysis, and the validity of the findings.

Synthesizing the literature: The researcher should identify patterns, themes, and relationships among the reviewed sources, and then synthesize the information into a coherent and logically organized narrative.

Identifying gaps and areas for further research: The literature review should highlight any gaps, inconsistencies, or areas that require further investigation, thereby informing the researcher's own study and contributing to the advancement of knowledge in the field.

Organizing and structuring the review: The literature review should be organized in a clear and logical manner, with sections and subsections that guide the reader through the key ideas and findings.

The literature review serves several important functions in the research process:

- It provides a solid foundation for the study by ensuring that the researcher is well-informed about the existing knowledge and current debates in the field.

- It helps to refine and sharpen the research question or hypothesis by identifying gaps or areas that warrant further investigation.

- It demonstrates the researcher's expertise and familiarity with the topic, which enhances the credibility of the study.

- It situates the current research within the broader context of the field and highlights its potential contribution.

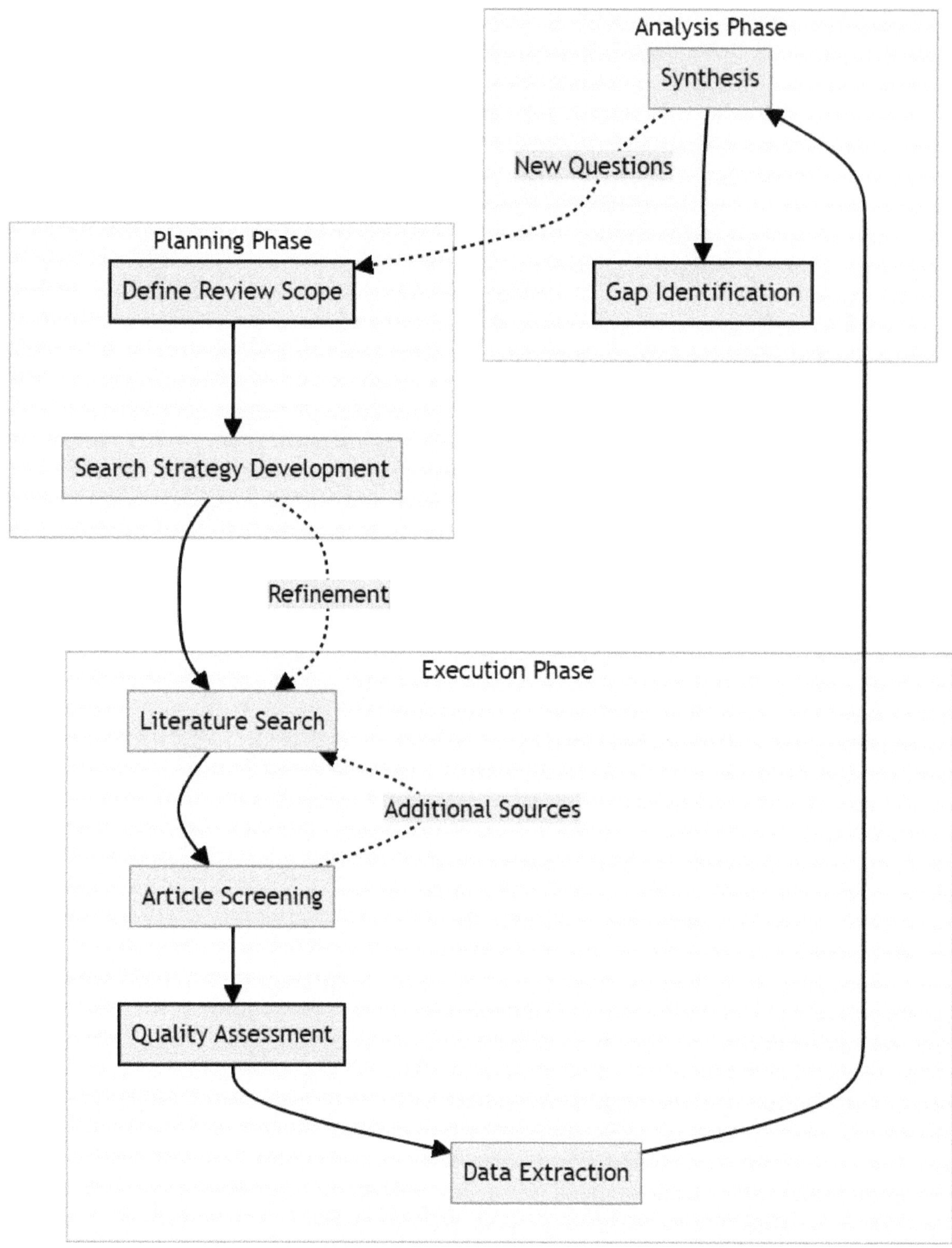

Fig. 2.2. Systematic Literature Review Process

By conducting a thorough and well-structured literature review, researchers can ensure that their study is grounded in a deep understanding of the existing literature and is ultimately more likely to make a meaningful contribution to the field of study.

The formulation of research questions represents the crystallization of identified gaps into specific, answerable queries.

Effective research questions should be:

1. **Specific**: Clearly defining the scope and focus of investigation

2. **Measurable**: Allowing for empirical investigation

3. **Achievable**: Feasible within available resources

4. **Relevant**: Contributing meaningfully to the field

5. **Time-bound**: Completable within a reasonable timeframe

For example, instead of asking "How does climate change affect marine life?" a well-formulated research question might be "What is the impact of a 2°C increase in water temperature on coral reef biodiversity in the Great Barrier Reef over a five-year period?"

2.5 Developing a Conceptual Framework

The development of a conceptual framework provides the theoretical foundation and structural support for research investigations. This framework serves as a bridge between theoretical concepts and practical research implementation.

Theoretical frameworks represent the established theories and models that inform research design and interpretation. They provide:

- Explanatory mechanisms for observed phenomena

- Predicted relationships between variables

- Theoretical context for new findings

- Basis for hypothesis generation

The conceptual framework builds upon theoretical foundations but focuses more specifically on the relationships and variables relevant to the current research. It serves several crucial functions:

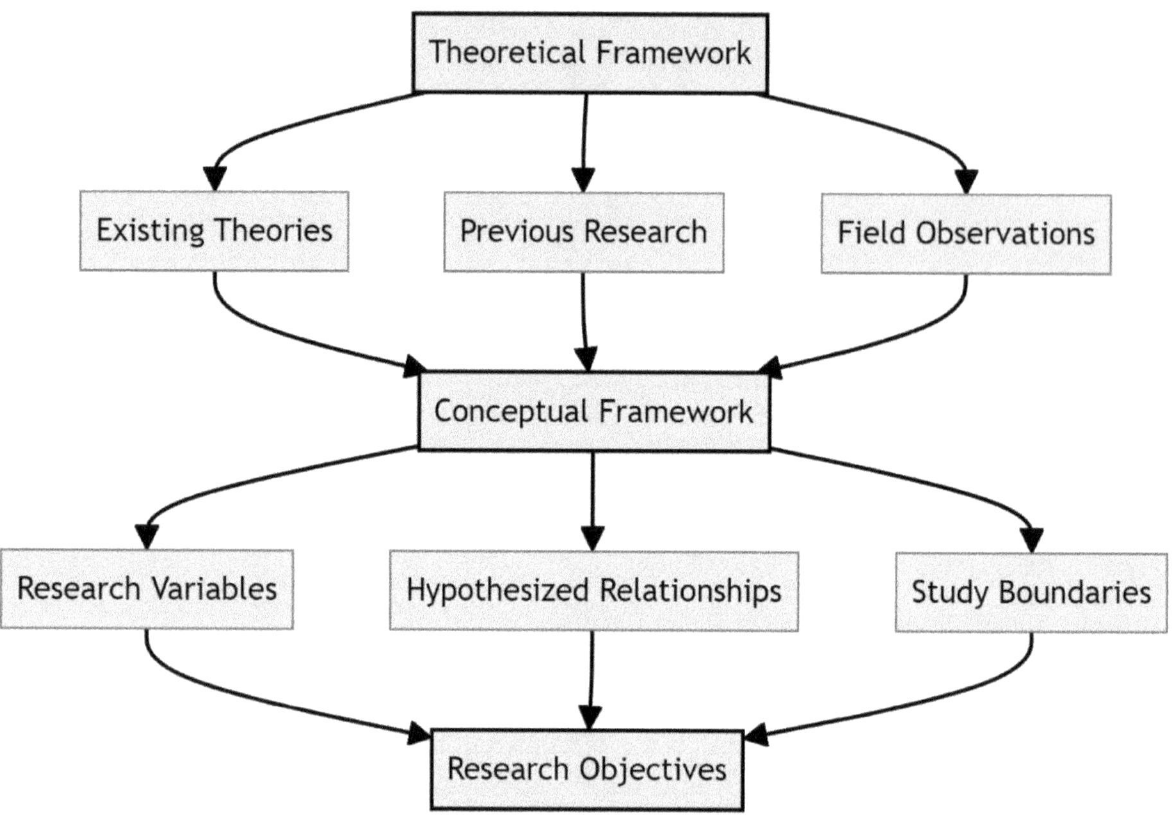

Fig. 2.3. Elements of Conceptual Framework Development

2.6 Organization of Ideas and Research Direction

Organization of Ideas

The organization of ideas in academic research represents a fundamental framework that enables researchers to systematically structure and analyze existing knowledge within their field of study. This crucial process encompasses several key elements, including the careful mapping of relationships between concepts, the identification of essential variables, the establishment of clear study boundaries, and the development of precise operational definitions. Through these interconnected components, researchers can effectively navigate the existing body of literature while creating a solid foundation for their own investigations. This systematic approach not only helps in understanding the current state of knowledge but also facilitates the identification of research gaps and the formation of well-defined research questions.

Mapping relationships between concepts: A well-structured literature review should effectively map the relationships between key concepts, theories, and findings within the research area. This involves identifying connections, interdependencies, and potential contradictions among the reviewed sources.

Identifying key variables: The literature review should highlight the primary variables, both independent and dependent, that are central to the research problem. This allows the researcher to understand how these variables have been previously examined and operationalized.

Establishing study boundaries: The literature review helps the researcher define the scope and boundaries of the study by clarifying what has been covered in previous research and what gaps or areas remain unexplored.

Defining operational definitions: The review of the literature should inform the development of clear and consistent operational definitions for the key concepts and variables involved in the research.

Research Direction

Research direction serves as a critical compass in academic investigation, providing essential guidance throughout the research process from conception to completion. By systematically reviewing and analyzing existing literature, researchers can develop well-informed hypotheses, select appropriate methodological approaches, determine effective data collection strategies, and identify suitable analytical frameworks. This comprehensive approach to research direction ensures that investigations are grounded in established knowledge while maintaining the flexibility to explore new perspectives and fill existing gaps in the literature. Through this structured process, researchers can maximize the effectiveness and relevance of their studies while maintaining alignment with accepted scientific practices and methodological standards.

Guiding hypothesis formation: The insights gained from the literature review can inform the formulation of research hypotheses by suggesting potential relationships, trends, or patterns that the current study can investigate.

Informing methodology selection: The literature review can guide the researcher in selecting appropriate research methods and designs that align with the existing knowledge base and address the identified gaps.

Directing data collection strategies: The review of the literature can help the researcher determine the most relevant and effective data collection techniques, sources, and instruments to address the research problem.

Structuring analysis approaches: The literature review can inform the selection and application of appropriate data analysis methods, statistical techniques, or interpretive frameworks that are well-suited to the research problem and the nature of the available data.

Setting research objectives flows naturally from well-developed conceptual frameworks.

Objectives should be:

Research Objectives Framework			
Objective Level	Characteristics	Example	Measurement Approach
Primary Objectives	• Core research goals • Direct link to main research question • Clear outcome measures	Determine the effect of drug X on blood pressure	• Primary outcome measures • Statistical hypothesis testing
Secondary Objectives	• Supporting goals • Related investigations • Additional insights	Assess side effects of drug X	• Secondary outcomes • Exploratory analyses
Operational Objectives	• Practical implementation goals • Process measures • Quality indicators	Achieve 90% participant retention	• Process metrics • Quality measures
Learning Objectives	• Knowledge generation goals • Capability development • Future research preparation	Develop validated measurement protocol	• Documentation quality • Protocol adoption

By carefully organizing the ideas and insights gained from the literature review, researchers can establish a strong foundation for their study. This, in turn, enhances the overall quality, coherence, and contribution of the research, as it ensures that the project is well-grounded in the existing knowledge and effectively addresses the identified gaps or areas of inquiry.

2.7 Research Design Selection

Research designs are the frameworks that guide the planning, implementation, and analysis of research studies. Three primary types of research designs are experimental, quasi-experimental, and observational. Each design has distinct characteristics and applications, offering researchers different approaches to investigating research questions and testing hypotheses.

2.7.1 Experimental Designs

Experimental designs are considered the gold standard for establishing causal relationships. They involve the random assignment of participants to different treatment conditions and the manipulation of one or more independent variables to observe their impact on the dependent variable(s).

The key features of experimental designs include:

1. ***Random assignment***: Participants are randomly assigned to different treatment groups, ensuring that any observed differences can be attributed to the independent variable(s) rather than pre-existing group differences.

2. ***Control group***: Experimental designs typically include a control group that receives a placebo or no treatment, allowing researchers to compare the effects of the intervention to a baseline condition.

3. ***Manipulation of independent variables***: Researchers actively manipulate the independent variable(s) to observe their impact on the dependent variable(s).

4. ***High internal validity***: Experimental designs have high internal validity, meaning they can establish causal relationships with a high degree of confidence due to the control over confounding variables.

Experimental designs are commonly used in fields such as psychology, medicine, and social sciences to test the effectiveness of interventions, treatments, or new programs. Examples include randomized controlled trials (RCTs) in clinical research and laboratory experiments in psychology.

2.7.2 Quasi-Experimental Designs

Quasi-experimental designs are similar to experimental designs but lack the element of random assignment. These designs are employed when random assignment is not feasible or ethical. Quasi-experimental designs maintain the manipulation of independent variables but lack the complete control over confounding variables that is present in true experimental designs.

The key features of quasi-experimental designs include:

1. ***Non-random assignment***: Participants are not randomly assigned to different conditions, but rather are assigned based on other factors, such as availability, preference, or existing group membership.

2. ***Comparison groups***: Quasi-experimental designs often include comparison groups, which are not randomly assigned but serve as a reference point for the treatment group(s).

3. ***Partially controlled confounding variables***: Quasi-experimental designs attempt to control for some confounding variables, but the lack of random assignment limits the ability to rule out all alternative explanations for observed effects.

4. ***Moderate internal validity***: Quasi-experimental designs have moderate internal validity, as the lack of random assignment introduces potential threats to validity, such as selection bias and history effects.

Quasi-experimental designs are commonly used in situations where random assignment is not feasible, such as in educational settings, community interventions, or when studying naturally occurring events. Examples include non-equivalent control group designs and time-series analyses.

2.7.3 Observational Designs

Observational designs do not involve the manipulation of independent variables but rather focus on observing and describing phenomena as they naturally occur. These designs do not attempt to establish causal relationships but rather explore associations and patterns.

The key features of observational designs include:

1. ***No intervention***: Researchers do not actively intervene or manipulate the independent variables. They observe and record the characteristics, behaviors, or events as they occur naturally.

2. ***Correlational analysis***: Observational designs often involve the analysis of relationships or associations between variables, without making claims about causality.

3. ***Naturalistic setting***: Observational studies are conducted in natural settings, such as in the field or in real-world environments, to capture the phenomenon of interest in its natural context.

4. ***Descriptive and exploratory***: Observational designs are primarily focused on describing and exploring the characteristics, patterns, and trends of the phenomenon under investigation.

5. ***Lower internal validity***: Observational designs have lower internal validity compared to experimental and quasi-experimental designs, as they lack the ability to establish causal relationships due to the absence of manipulation and random assignment.

Observational designs are commonly used in fields such as anthropology, sociology, and epidemiology to study human behavior, social interactions, and natural occurrences. Examples include case studies, ethnographic research, and cohort studies.

Research Design Selection Framework			
Selection Criteria	**Considerations**	**Impact on Design Choice**	**Examples**
Research Objectives	• Causal inference needs • Descriptive vs. analytical goals • Hypothesis testing requirements	Determines basic design approach	Testing drug efficacy requires experimental design
Internal Validity	• Control over variables • Randomization possibility • Confounding factor control	Influences design rigor	Laboratory studies maximize control
External Validity	• Generalizability needs • Real-world applicability • Population representation	Affects study setting and sample selection	Field studies increase external validity
Resource Constraints	• Budget limitations • Time constraints • Available expertise	Determines feasible design options	Cost constraints might favor observational designs
Ethical Considerations	• Risk to participants • Control group justification • Intervention safety	May limit design options	Cannot randomize harmful exposures
Practical Feasibility	• Access to participants • Technology requirements • Implementation challenges	Influences design complexity	Remote locations might require simplified designs

The choice of research design depends on the research question, the feasibility of the study, ethical considerations, and the level of control the researcher can exert over the variables of interest. Experimental designs provide the strongest evidence for causal relationships, while quasi-experimental and observational designs offer valuable insights into real-world phenomena and can be used to generate hypotheses for future experimental investigations.

2.8 Trade-offs

Researchers face important trade-offs when choosing between experimental, quasi-experimental, and observational research designs. Each approach offers distinct advantages and limitations that must be carefully weighed.

Experimental designs provide the strongest evidence for causal relationships by allowing researchers to actively manipulate independent variables and randomly assign participants. This high level of control enhances internal validity, but can limit generalizability to real-world settings.

Quasi-experimental designs sacrifice some internal validity by lacking random assignment, yet can yield insights more applicable to natural contexts. The ability to study intact groups makes them suitable for field research.

Observational studies forgo manipulation to examine phenomena as they naturally occur. While weaker for causal inference, observational methods can uncover unexpected patterns and generate hypotheses for future experimentation.

Trade-offs exist between rigor, feasibility, and ecological validity. Researchers must balance scientific standards with practical constraints and the needs of the research question. Careful consideration of these factors is crucial when selecting an appropriate research design.

2.9 Planning the Research Process

Effective project management in research requires careful attention to timeline development, resource allocation, and coordination of various activities. The success of a research project often depends as much on careful planning and management as on scientific merit.

Effective project management in research settings requires careful attention to several interconnected components that collectively ensure project success and scientific rigor. The development of comprehensive timelines stands as a foundational element, demanding meticulous planning to accommodate various research phases while building in flexibility for inevitable delays and adjustments. These timelines must align with funding cycles, academic calendars, and participant availability, creating a robust framework that guides project progression while maintaining adaptability.

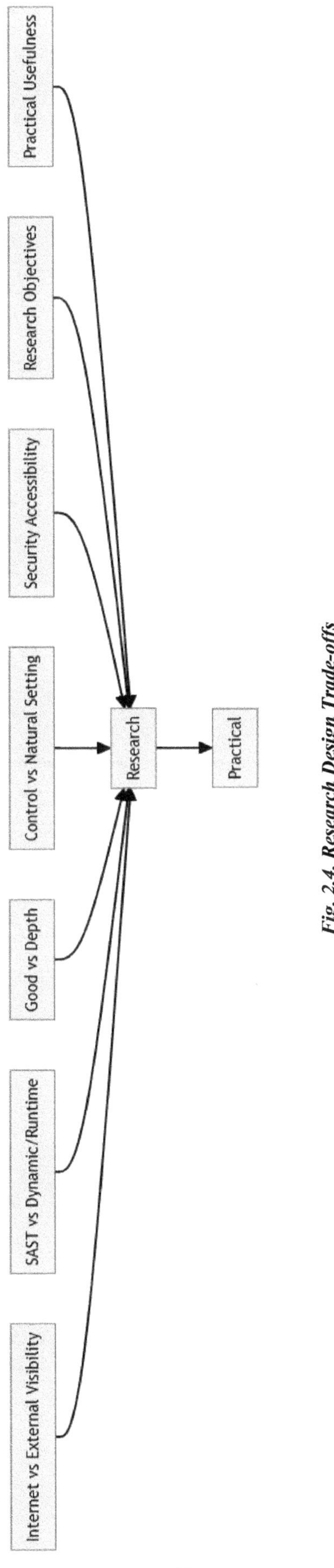

Fig. 2.4. Research Design Trade-offs

2.9.1 Budget planning

Budget planning represents another critical component, encompassing both direct and indirect costs that impact project feasibility and sustainability. Direct costs include essential elements such as personnel salaries, benefits, equipment purchases, laboratory fees, participant compensation, and travel expenses. These tangible expenses are complemented by indirect costs, including facility overhead, administrative support, insurance coverage, and contingency funds. Successful research projects require careful balance between these cost categories, ensuring adequate resources while maintaining fiscal responsibility.

2.9.2 Resource planning

Resource planning emerges as a multifaceted challenge, demanding attention to human, physical, and information resources. Human resources management involves assembling and maintaining an effective research team, clearly defining roles and responsibilities, addressing training requirements, and establishing backup personnel plans to ensure continuity. Physical resources encompass laboratory space, equipment, computing facilities, storage solutions, and specialized instruments necessary for research execution. Information resources, equally crucial, include database access, software licenses, reference materials, and technical support systems that facilitate data collection, analysis, and interpretation.

2.9.3 Quality management

Quality management serves as the backbone of research integrity, establishing standards and procedures that ensure reliable, reproducible results. This component requires implementing rigorous protocols, maintaining detailed documentation, conducting regular audits, and establishing clear communication channels among team members. Quality management systems must address data collection, storage, analysis, and reporting, while also ensuring compliance with relevant regulatory requirements and ethical standards.

2.9.4 Risk management

Risk management emerges as a critical component that safeguards project continuity and success. Technical risks, including equipment failure, methodological challenges, and technical difficulties, must be anticipated and addressed through preventive measures and contingency planning. Operational risks encompass personnel turnover, resource unavailability, and timeline delays, requiring flexible management strategies and robust backup plans. External risks, including funding changes, regulatory modifications, and environmental factors, demand ongoing monitoring and adaptive responses to maintain project momentum.

The integration of these components requires strategic coordination and regular assessment to ensure alignment with project objectives. Research leaders must maintain clear communication channels, establish feedback mechanisms, and implement adaptive management strategies that respond to changing conditions while preserving scientific integrity. This comprehensive approach to project management supports both immediate research goals and long-term scientific advancement, creating a foundation for successful project execution and meaningful contributions to the field.

Effective project management in research settings also demands attention to cross-component interactions and dependencies. Timeline development must account for budget constraints, resource availability, and risk factors, creating a realistic framework for project execution. Similarly, budget planning must consider resource requirements, quality management needs, and risk mitigation strategies, ensuring adequate funding for all project aspects. This interconnected approach strengthens project resilience and adapts to challenges while maintaining scientific rigor and research quality.

The success of research project management ultimately depends on the careful orchestration of these components, supported by clear communication, regular assessment, and adaptive management strategies. Project leaders must maintain a balanced perspective, addressing immediate operational needs while preserving long-term research objectives. This comprehensive approach to project management creates a robust framework for scientific investigation, supporting both research excellence and operational efficiency in advancing knowledge and understanding within their field.

Quality Management Strategies			
Quality Component	**Implementation Strategies**	**Monitoring Methods**	**Corrective Actions**
Data Quality	• Standardized collection protocols • Training programs • Quality control checks	• Regular audits • Statistical monitoring • Validation checks	• Protocol revision • Retraining • Data cleaning
Process Quality	• Standard operating procedures • Workflow documentation • Clear responsibilities	• Process audits • Timeline tracking • Milestone reviews	• Process optimization • Resource reallocation • Timeline adjustment
Output Quality	• Peer review processes • Quality metrics • Validation procedures	• Expert review • Quality scoring • Benchmarking	• Revision cycles • Additional analysis • External consultation
Team Quality	• Training programs • Performance standards • Communication protocols	• Performance reviews • Team assessments • Skill evaluations	• Additional training • Role reassignment • Team restructuring

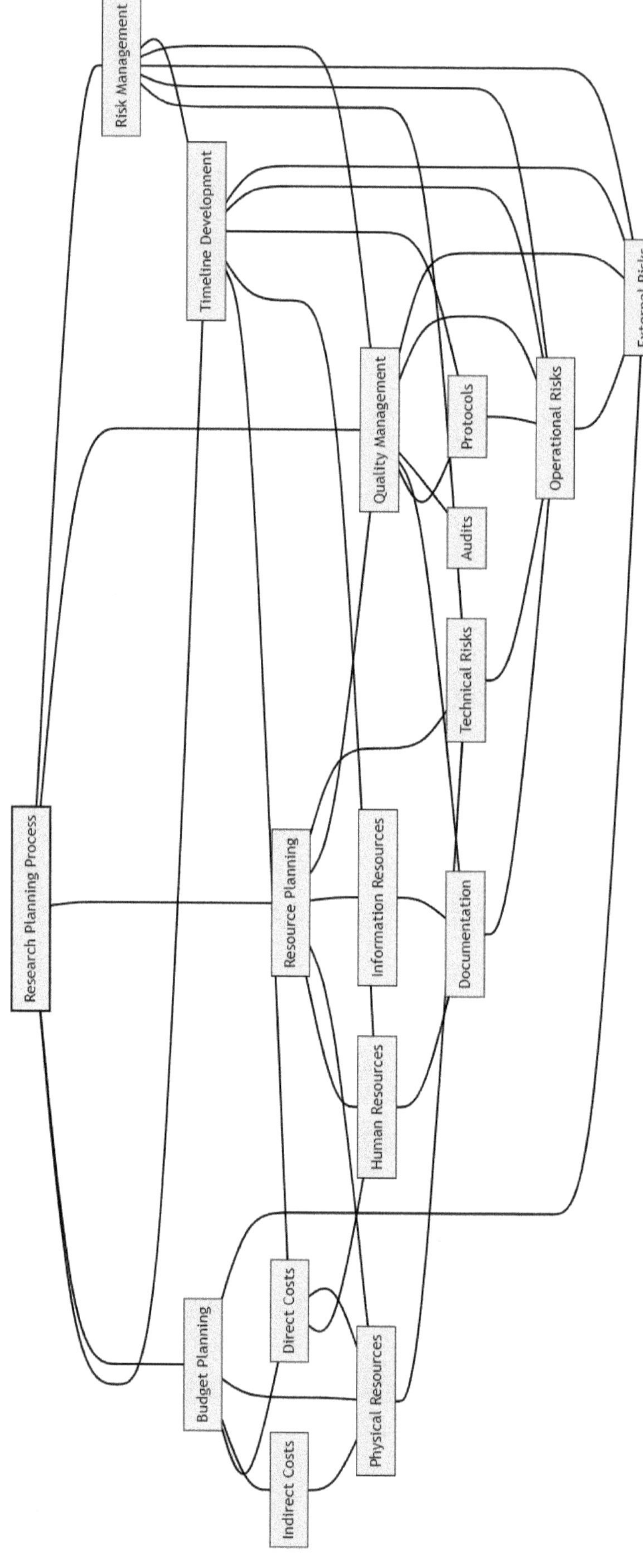

Fig. 2.5. Research Planning Process

3. Data Collection Techniques

The important thing is not to stop questioning. Curiosity has its own reason for existing.

- *Albert Einstein*

In life sciences research, the quality and reliability of findings depend heavily on the methods used to collect data. This chapter explores various data collection techniques, their applications, and considerations for their effective implementation in research studies.

3.1 Data Collection in Life Sciences

Data collection in life sciences forms the cornerstone of biological research, requiring meticulous planning and execution to ensure scientific validity. The process encompasses various methodologies ranging from molecular analysis to organism-level observations, each demanding specific protocols and quality controls to maintain data integrity.

3.1.1 Types of Data

Quantitative data collection in life sciences involves precise measurements of biological parameters, including gene expression levels, protein concentrations, metabolic rates, and physiological responses. These measurements often utilize sophisticated instrumentation such as spectrophotometers, flow cytometers, and mass spectrometers, requiring careful calibration and standardization protocols. Researchers must establish clear parameters for data recording, including units of measurement, sampling intervals, and environmental conditions that might influence results.

Qualitative observations play an equally crucial role, particularly in behavioral studies, morphological analysis, and ecological surveys. These observations require standardized recording methods to minimize observer bias and ensure reproducibility. Researchers often develop detailed rubrics or scoring systems to convert qualitative observations into quantifiable data points, facilitating statistical analysis and interpretation.

Field-based data collection introduces additional complexities, requiring researchers to account for environmental variables and seasonal variations. This might involve tracking weather conditions, soil composition, or population dynamics across different ecosystems. Mobile data collection tools and GPS tracking systems have revolutionized field research, enabling real-time data recording and spatial analysis of biological phenomena.

Laboratory-based data collection demands strict adherence to experimental protocols and careful documentation of procedural variations. This includes maintaining detailed records of reagent preparations, equipment settings, and environmental conditions that might affect experimental outcomes. Modern laboratory information management systems (LIMS) facilitate this process, enabling systematic data organization and retrieval.

Digital data collection has become increasingly prevalent, generating massive datasets through techniques like next-generation sequencing, proteomics, and high-throughput screening. These methods require robust data management systems and quality control measures to handle large volumes of information while maintaining data integrity. Researchers must also consider data storage formats, backup procedures, and accessibility requirements for long-term data preservation.

3.1.2 Ethics and Quality Assurance

Ethics in data collection remains paramount, particularly when working with human subjects or animal models. Researchers must obtain appropriate institutional approvals, maintain participant confidentiality, and ensure compliance with regulatory requirements. This includes proper documentation of informed consent procedures and careful handling of sensitive personal information.

Quality assurance in data collection involves implementing various control measures throughout the research process. This includes using appropriate controls in experimental designs, conducting regular equipment calibration, and maintaining detailed documentation of any deviations from standard protocols. Researchers must also establish clear procedures for identifying and handling outliers or anomalous data points.

3.1.3 Data validation

Data validation represents a critical step in the collection process, requiring researchers to verify the accuracy and consistency of recorded information. This might involve cross-checking measurements, performing statistical analyses to identify potential errors, and validating results through independent replication. Modern data collection platforms often incorporate automated validation checks to flag potential inconsistencies or errors in real-time.

The future of data collection in life sciences continues to evolve with technological advances, incorporating artificial intelligence and machine learning tools for automated data collection and analysis. These developments promise to enhance the efficiency and accuracy of data collection while presenting new challenges in data management and interpretation. Researchers must stay informed about emerging technologies and best practices to ensure their data collection methods remain current and effective.

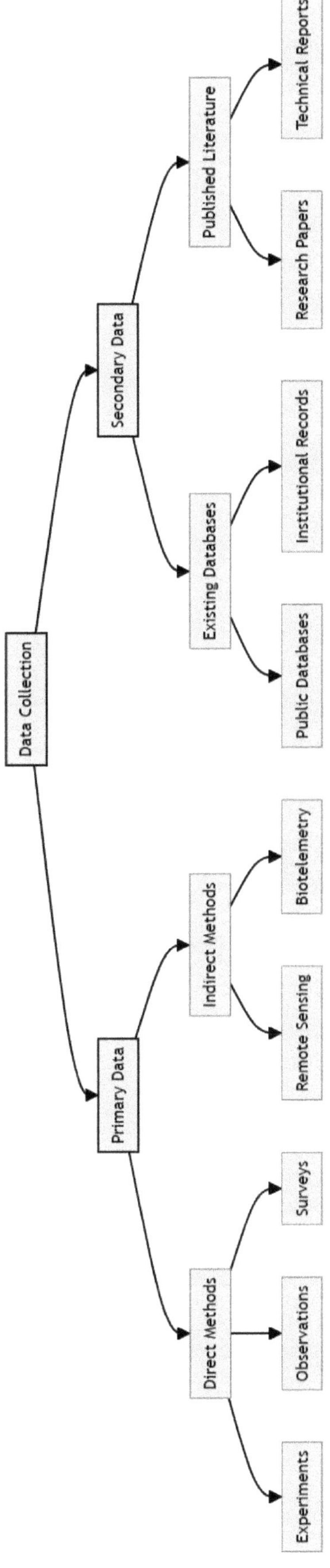

Fig. 3.1. Data Collection Framework in Life Sciences

Primary vs Secondary Data Source Comparison			
Characteristic	**Primary Data**	**Secondary Data**	**Implications**
Data Collection Control	High - Research team determines collection methods	Low - Must work with existing methods	Affects reliability and validity assessments
Resource Requirements	High - Requires significant time and resources	Lower - Data already exists	Influences project planning and budgeting
Timeliness	Current - Data collected for specific study	Historical - May be outdated	Impacts relevance and generalizability
Specificity	High - Tailored to research questions	Variable - May require adaptation	Affects analysis approach and interpretation
Quality Control	Direct - Team maintains standards	Indirect - Dependent on original collectors	Influences confidence in findings
Access Issues	Controlled - Direct access to raw data	Variable - May have restrictions	Affects feasibility and timeline
Ethical Considerations	Direct - Requires full ethical review	Modified - May need secondary approval	Impacts study design and implementation
Scope	Limited - Typically focused on specific questions	Broad - May cover multiple aspects	Influences research question development

3.2 Primary Data Collection Methods

Primary data collection methods represent the foundational approaches researchers use to gather original information directly from sources. These methods, essential across various scientific disciplines, require careful planning and execution to ensure data quality and reliability.

Surveys and **questionnaires** serve as fundamental tools for gathering structured data from large populations. These instruments can be administered through various channels, including online platforms, mail, telephone, or in-person interviews. Effective survey design requires clear, unambiguous questions, appropriate response formats, and careful consideration of sampling methods to ensure representative results.

Interviews provide deeper insights through direct interaction with subjects. Structured interviews follow predetermined questions, while semi-structured and unstructured interviews allow for more flexible exploration of topics. These methods prove particularly valuable when seeking detailed explanations, personal experiences, or expert opinions. Interviewers must maintain objectivity while building rapport with participants to elicit honest, comprehensive responses.

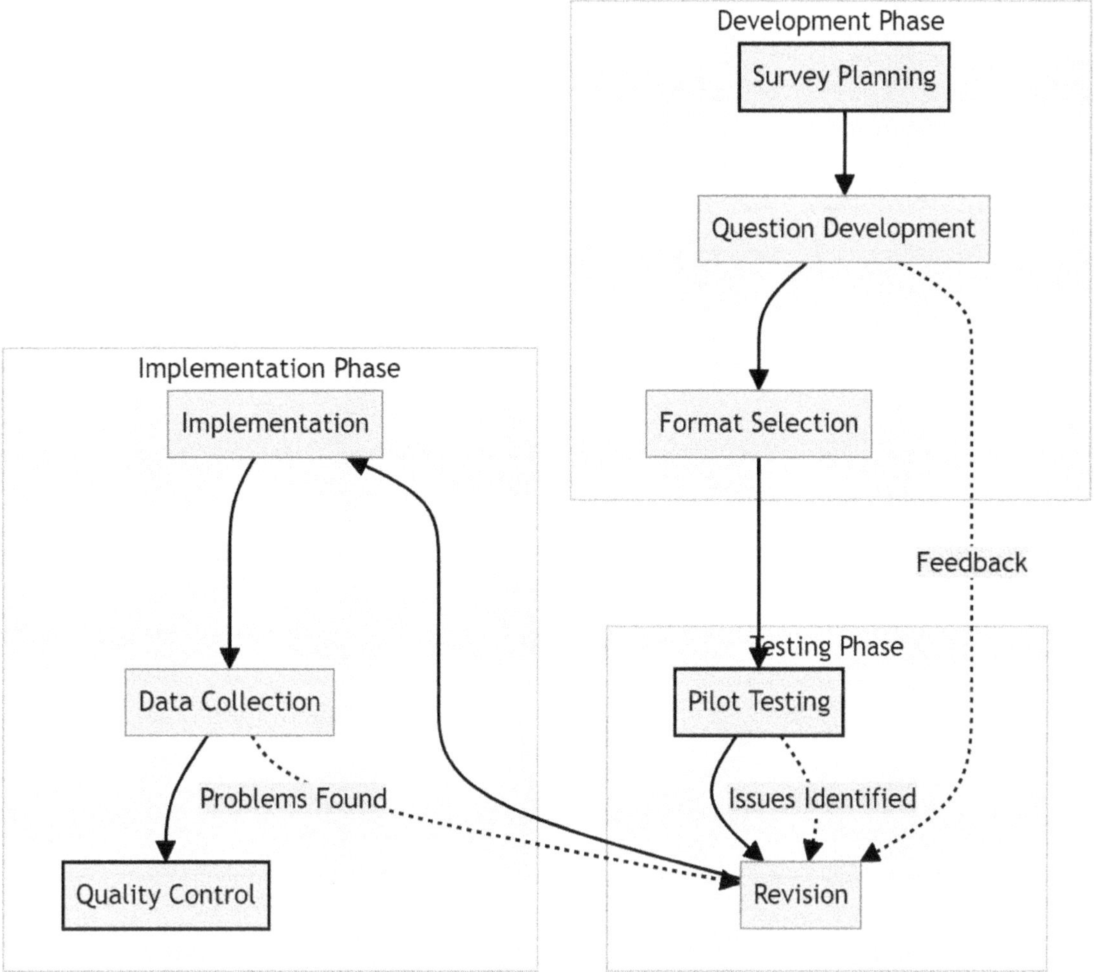

Fig. 3.2. Survey Development and Implementation Process

Observational studies involve systematic monitoring and recording of phenomena in natural settings. This method proves invaluable in behavioral research, ecological studies, and social sciences. Researchers may employ various observation techniques, from direct observation with detailed field notes to video recording for later analysis. The key challenge lies in minimizing observer bias while capturing relevant behavioral patterns and interactions.

Experimental methods involve manipulating variables under controlled conditions to establish cause-and-effect relationships. This approach requires careful experimental design, including proper control groups, randomization, and replication. Researchers must account for potential confounding variables and ensure proper documentation of all experimental conditions and procedures.

Field research combines multiple data collection methods in natural settings. This approach often integrates observational data with environmental measurements, sampling procedures, and in-situ testing. Field researchers must adapt to changing conditions while maintaining methodological rigor and data quality standards.

Laboratory analysis provides quantitative data through specialized equipment and controlled testing procedures. This method requires strict adherence to protocols, proper calibration of instruments, and careful documentation of procedures. Quality control measures, including proper sample handling and storage, prove essential for reliable results.

Focus groups facilitate collective discussion and interaction among participants, generating insights through group dynamics. This method proves particularly useful for exploring perceptions, attitudes, and responses to new concepts or products. Moderators must balance group interaction with individual participation while maintaining discussion focus.

Case studies involve comprehensive examination of specific instances or phenomena, often combining multiple data collection methods. This approach provides detailed understanding of complex situations through thorough documentation and analysis. Researchers must establish clear boundaries while gathering sufficient evidence to support conclusions.

Documentation analysis involves examining existing records, reports, and artifacts. This method provides historical context and supports triangulation with other data sources. Researchers must verify document authenticity and account for potential biases in recorded information.

3.3 Secondary Data Collection Methods

Secondary data collection methods involve the analysis and interpretation of existing data gathered by other researchers or organizations. These methods provide cost-effective access to large datasets while requiring careful evaluation of data quality and relevance.

Government databases represent a primary source of secondary data, offering comprehensive datasets on demographics, economic indicators, health statistics, and environmental measurements. These repositories typically maintain high data quality standards but may have limitations in terms of update frequency and specific variable availability.

Academic research databases provide access to peer-reviewed studies, experimental results, and analysis across various disciplines. These sources often include raw data supplements, methodological details, and analytical frameworks that support research replication and meta-analysis. Researchers must carefully evaluate study methodologies and potential biases when utilizing these resources.

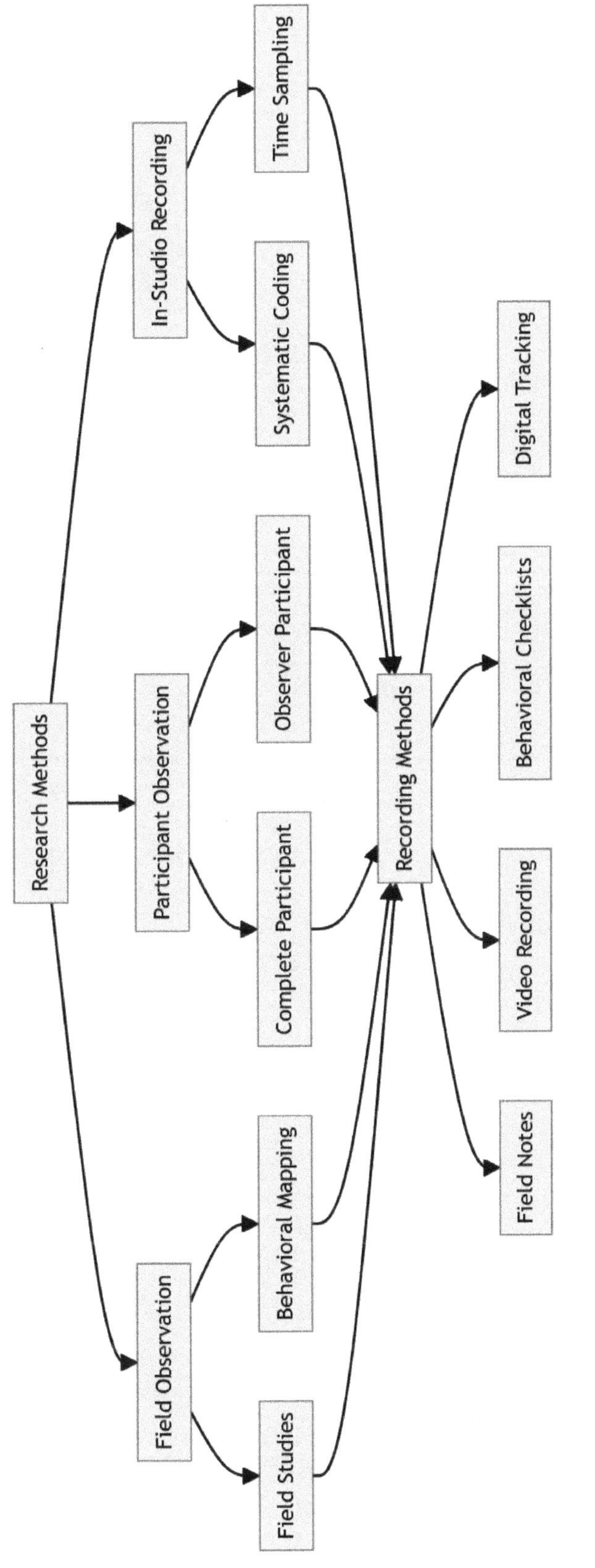

Fig. 3.3. Types of Observational Techniques

Secondary Data Sources and Considerations				
Data Source Type	**Examples**	**Advantages**	**Challenges**	**Quality Considerations**
Public Databases	GenBank, PubMed, GBIF	• Wide coverage • Standardized format • Free access	• Data currency • Format compatibility • Missing values	• Data validation • Source reputation • Update frequency
Institutional Records	Hospital records, Laboratory logs	• Detailed information • Long-term data • Professional collection	• Access restrictions • Privacy concerns • Format inconsistency	• Collection methods • Record completeness • Documentation quality
Research Archives	Previous studies, Historical data	• Rich context • Established methodology • Known limitations	• Outdated methods • Technology changes • Lost documentation	• Original purpose • Collection context • Methodology details
Government Data	Census, Environmental monitoring	• Large scale • Regular updates • Official source	• Aggregation level • Political influence • Release delays	• Collection standards • Reporting methods • Verification processes

Industry reports and **market analyses** offer insights into business trends, consumer behavior, and technological developments. While these sources may provide valuable sector-specific information, researchers should consider potential commercial biases and verify data through multiple sources when possible.

Historical records and **archives** contain valuable longitudinal data that can reveal patterns and trends over extended periods. These sources require careful authentication and consideration of historical context in data interpretation. Digital archives have improved accessibility while raising questions about data preservation and format compatibility.

International organizations maintain extensive databases covering global trends in health, economics, education, and environmental indicators. These sources often provide standardized data across multiple countries, though differences in collection methods and reporting standards must be considered.

Social media and digital platforms generate vast amounts of behavioral and interaction data. While offering real-time insights into social phenomena, these sources present challenges in data quality verification and ethical considerations regarding privacy and consent.

Clinical and **healthcare records** provide detailed patient data useful for medical research and epidemiological studies. Access to these sources requires strict adherence to privacy regulations and careful consideration of patient confidentiality.

Census data offers comprehensive demographic and socioeconomic information at various geographical levels. Though highly reliable, researchers must account for collection intervals and potential undercounting in certain populations.

Meteorological and **environmental monitoring systems** provide continuous data on climate patterns and environmental conditions. These sources often offer historical trends useful for environmental research, though data consistency across different monitoring systems requires verification.

Challenges in accessing and using secondary data

Accessing and collecting secondary data presents researchers with numerous complex challenges that can impact research quality and validity. Data accessibility often poses a significant barrier, with many valuable datasets restricted behind paywalls, institutional memberships, or proprietary systems. This limitation can create disparities in research capabilities between well-funded institutions and those with limited resources.

Data quality verification presents another critical challenge, as researchers must assess the reliability and validity of data collected by others. This includes evaluating the original collection methodology, identifying potential biases, and understanding any limitations in the dataset. Missing or incomplete data points, inconsistent recording methods, and changes in collection procedures over time can compromise data integrity.

Format compatibility and technological barriers frequently complicate secondary data utilization. Historical datasets may exist in obsolete formats or require significant preprocessing before analysis. Different organizations often use varying data structures, coding systems, and measurement units, necessitating careful standardization and conversion processes.

Privacy regulations and ethical considerations significantly impact access to sensitive data, particularly in healthcare and social research. Compliance with data protection laws, such as GDPR or HIPAA, requires careful navigation of legal requirements and often lengthy approval processes. Anonymization and data security measures may limit the granularity of available information.

Data currency and timeliness pose challenges when research requires recent information. Many secondary sources experience lag times between data collection and publication, potentially affecting the relevance of findings. Regular updates to datasets may also introduce inconsistencies in longitudinal studies.

Documentation quality varies significantly across secondary sources, with some lacking crucial information about collection methods, variable definitions, or data cleaning procedures. This inadequate documentation can make it difficult to assess data suitability for specific research questions or replicate previous analyses.

Licensing and usage restrictions often limit how secondary data can be utilized and shared. Researchers must navigate complex terms of use, attribution requirements, and restrictions on data modification or redistribution. These constraints can impact research transparency and replication efforts.

Cultural and linguistic barriers may affect interpretation of international datasets. Variations in cultural contexts, terminology, and measurement practices across different regions require careful consideration during data analysis and interpretation.

Cost considerations extend beyond initial access fees to include expenses for data storage, processing tools, and specialized software required for analysis. Long-term storage and maintenance of large secondary datasets can strain institutional resources and infrastructure.

Bias in secondary data represents a persistent challenge, whether from selection bias in the original collection process, reporting bias in official statistics, or systematic exclusion of certain populations. Researchers must carefully evaluate and account for these biases in their analyses and conclusions.

3.4 Data Collection in Qualitative vs. Quantitative Research

Data collection approaches differ significantly between qualitative and quantitative research methodologies, each serving distinct research objectives and epistemological foundations. Quantitative research focuses on numerical data and statistical analysis, employing structured collection methods that prioritize objectivity and standardization. These methods typically include surveys with closed-ended questions, structured observations, experimental measurements, and standardized tests, all designed to generate data that can be statistically analyzed.

Quantitative data collection emphasizes reliability and replicability, utilizing precise measurement tools and controlled environments. Researchers employ random sampling techniques to ensure representativeness and minimize bias. Data collection instruments are typically validated before use, with clear protocols for administration and scoring. This approach allows for hypothesis testing, variable manipulation, and the identification of causal relationships through statistical analysis.

In contrast, qualitative research focuses on understanding meanings, experiences, and contexts through rich, descriptive data. Collection methods include in-depth interviews, participant observation, focus groups, and document analysis. These approaches allow researchers to explore complex phenomena in natural settings, capturing nuanced perspectives and contextual details that might be missed in quantitative studies.

Qualitative data collection typically involves smaller sample sizes but generates more detailed information per participant. Researchers often use purposive sampling to identify information-rich cases rather than aiming for statistical representativeness. The collection process is usually more flexible and iterative, allowing researchers to adapt their approach based on emerging insights and themes.

The role of the researcher also differs significantly between these approaches. In quantitative research, investigators strive to maintain objective distance from subjects, using standardized procedures to minimize personal influence on data collection. Qualitative researchers, however, often serve as the primary data collection instrument, actively engaging with participants and acknowledging their own role in the research process.

Data analysis approaches reflect these methodological differences. Quantitative data analysis employs statistical techniques to test hypotheses and identify patterns, while qualitative analysis involves thematic coding and interpretation to understand meanings and contexts. Many contemporary researchers recognize the value of mixing these approaches, combining quantitative and qualitative methods to provide more comprehensive understanding of research questions.

Time and resource requirements vary between these approaches. Quantitative data collection often requires larger sample sizes but can be completed more quickly through standardized procedures. Qualitative data collection typically takes longer per participant but may require fewer subjects overall. Both approaches demand careful attention to ethical considerations, including informed consent, confidentiality, and potential impact on participants.

Technology plays an increasingly important role in both types of data collection. Digital surveys and automated data capture systems facilitate quantitative data collection, while qualitative researchers utilize recording devices, transcription software, and qualitative data analysis programs. These tools can enhance efficiency and accuracy while introducing new considerations for data security and participant privacy.

Quality assurance measures differ between approaches. Quantitative research emphasizes statistical validity, reliability, and generalizability, employing various controls and standardization procedures. Qualitative research focuses on trustworthiness, credibility, and transferability, often using techniques like member checking, triangulation, and thick description to ensure research quality.

The choice between qualitative and quantitative approaches ultimately depends on research objectives, questions, and theoretical frameworks. Many researchers advocate for mixed-methods approaches that leverage the strengths of both methodologies, providing more comprehensive understanding of complex phenomena while addressing the limitations inherent in each approach.

3.5 Mixed Methods Approaches in Life Sciences

Mixed methods research in life sciences combines quantitative and qualitative approaches to provide comprehensive understanding of biological phenomena. This integration allows researchers to capture both measurable data and contextual insights, particularly valuable in complex biological systems and their interactions with environmental and social factors.

The sequential explanatory design represents a common approach where quantitative data collection precedes qualitative investigation. For example, researchers might analyze population genetics data quantitatively before conducting qualitative interviews with conservation managers to understand implementation challenges of breeding programs.

Concurrent triangulation designs involve simultaneous collection of quantitative and qualitative data. In ecological studies, this might combine quantitative measurements of species abundance with qualitative observations of animal behavior patterns. The simultaneous collection allows researchers to cross-validate findings and identify discrepancies requiring further investigation.

Embedded designs incorporate secondary methodology within a primary approach. For instance, a primarily quantitative clinical trial might include qualitative interviews with a subset of participants to understand treatment adherence challenges. This design provides depth to statistical findings while maintaining the rigorous structure of clinical research.

Integration challenges in mixed methods require careful consideration of data compatibility and analysis approaches. Researchers must develop frameworks for combining numerical data with observational insights while maintaining scientific rigor. This often involves creating coding systems that bridge quantitative and qualitative findings.

Technology integration plays a crucial role in modern mixed methods research. Advanced software platforms enable simultaneous collection and analysis of different data types, while machine learning algorithms can help identify patterns across diverse datasets. These tools support more sophisticated integration of quantitative and qualitative insights.

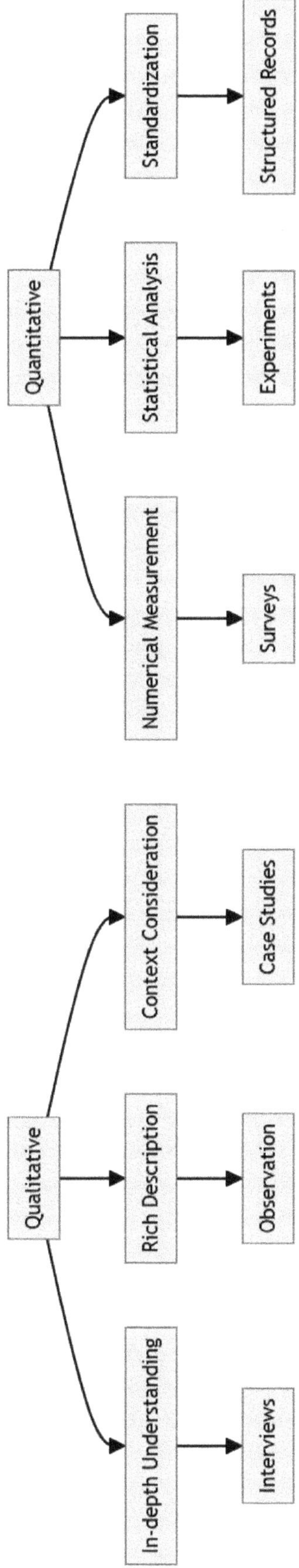

Fig. 3.4. Qualitative vs Quantitative Data Collection

Validation strategies in mixed methods research often employ multiple triangulation approaches. These might include methodological triangulation (comparing results from different methods), data triangulation (using different data sources), and investigator triangulation (involving multiple researchers in analysis).

The temporal dimension of mixed methods research requires careful planning. Some studies employ iterative designs where initial findings inform subsequent data collection phases. This flexibility allows researchers to adapt their approach based on emerging insights while maintaining methodological rigor.

Quality assurance in mixed methods combines standards from both quantitative and qualitative traditions. This includes statistical validity measures alongside qualitative credibility checks, requiring researchers to maintain high standards across different methodological approaches.

Ethical considerations in mixed methods research must address requirements for both quantitative and qualitative approaches. This includes ensuring informed consent covers all data collection methods while protecting participant confidentiality across different types of data.

4. Measurement and Scaling Techniques

Research is what I'm doing when I don't know what I'm doing.

-   Wernher von Braun

The foundation of scientific research lies in its ability to accurately measure and quantify phenomena. In life sciences, the complexity of biological systems makes precise measurement particularly crucial yet challenging. This chapter explores the fundamental concepts and techniques of measurement in research.

4.1 Understanding Measurement in Research

Measurement in research encompasses the systematic assignment of values to observations, requiring precise methodology to ensure accuracy and reliability. The foundation of scientific measurement rests on four key measurement scales: nominal, ordinal, interval, and ratio, each offering different levels of mathematical operations and statistical analysis possibilities.

4.1.1 Nominal measurement

Nominal measurement represents the most basic level, involving categorization without numerical significance. In biological research, this might include classification of species, gender assignment, or habitat types. While limited to frequency counts and mode calculations, nominal measurements provide essential categorical data for research organization.

4.1.2 Ordinal measurements

Ordinal measurements introduce ranking capabilities, allowing researchers to arrange observations in meaningful order while maintaining unequal intervals between ranks. Common applications include disease severity scales, ecosystem health rankings, or behavioral intensity measurements. These measurements support median calculations and non-parametric statistical analyses.

4.1.3 Interval measurements

Interval measurements provide equal distances between values but lack a true zero point. Temperature measurements in Celsius or Fahrenheit exemplify this scale, allowing for addition and subtraction operations. This level enables more sophisticated statistical analyses, including means and standard deviations, crucial for many biological studies.

4.1.4 Ratio measurements

Ratio measurements incorporate all properties of previous scales while including a meaningful zero point. Examples include weight, length, or concentration measurements in laboratory studies. This scale permits all mathematical operations and supports comprehensive statistical analysis, making it particularly valuable in quantitative research.

4.1.5 Measurement error

Measurement error represents a critical consideration in research design. Systematic errors introduce consistent bias in measurements, while random errors create unpredictable variations. Researchers must implement calibration procedures, standardization protocols, and quality control measures to minimize these errors.

4.1.6 Reliability

Reliability in measurement encompasses consistency across repeated observations. Test-retest reliability, inter-rater reliability, and internal consistency become crucial considerations when developing measurement protocols. Regular instrument calibration, standardized procedures, and proper training help maintain measurement reliability.

4.1.7 Validity

Validity ensures measurements accurately represent intended concepts or phenomena. Content validity, construct validity, and criterion validity must be established through careful instrument design and validation studies. This becomes particularly important in complex biological systems where direct measurement may be challenging.

Precision and **accuracy** represent distinct but related measurement concepts. Precision refers to measurement consistency, while accuracy indicates closeness to true values. Research design must balance these considerations based on study objectives and available resources.

Advanced measurement technologies continue to evolve, introducing new capabilities and challenges. Digital sensors, automated data collection systems, and real-time monitoring devices enhance measurement precision while requiring careful validation and calibration protocols.

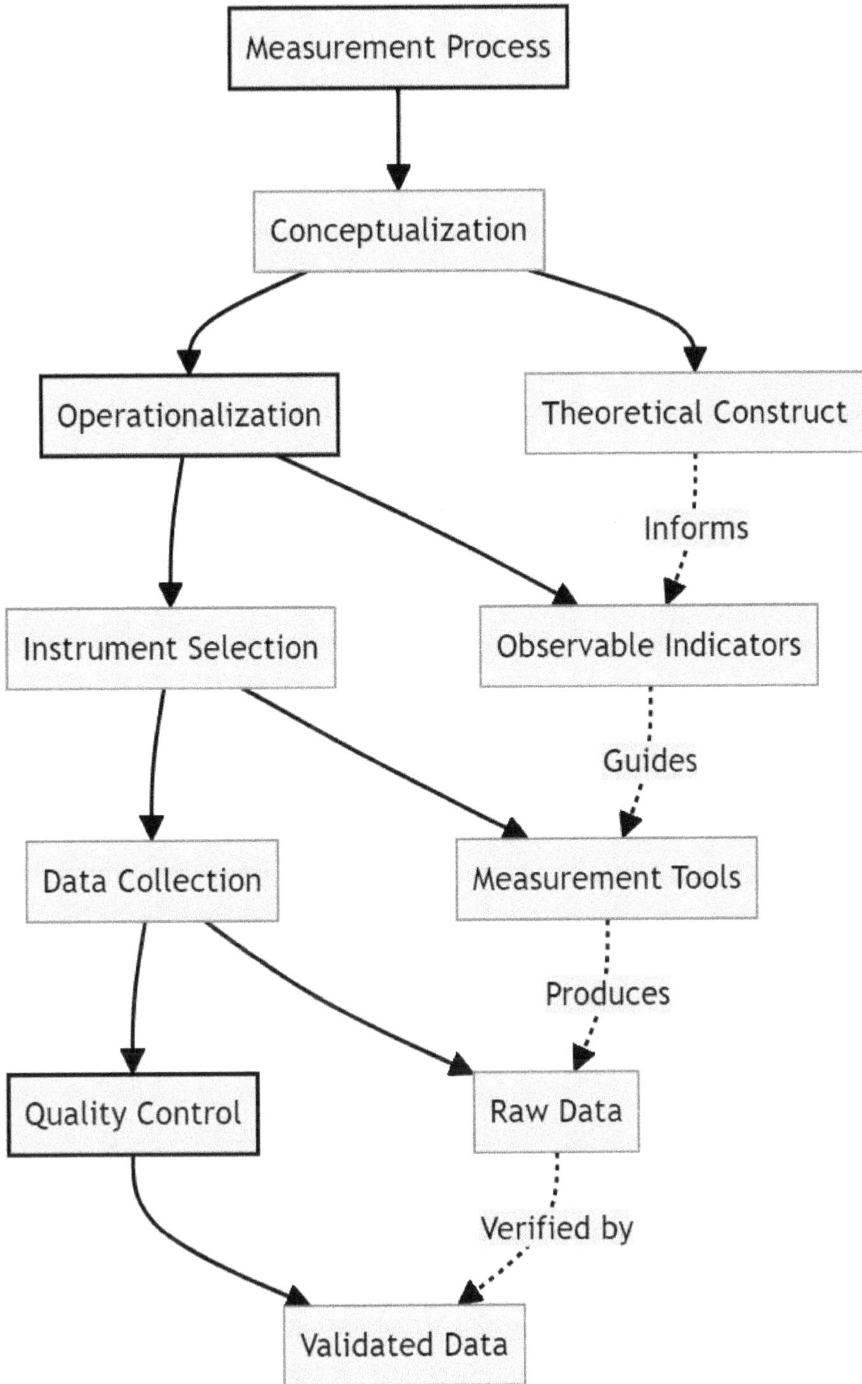

Fig. 4.1. Research Measurement Framework

The importance of accurate measurement in life sciences cannot be overstated. Accurate measurement in life sciences forms the cornerstone of reliable research and scientific advancement. In molecular biology, precise measurements of protein concentrations, gene expression levels, and enzymatic activities directly impact experimental reproducibility and validity. Even minor measurement errors can propagate through experiments, potentially leading to incorrect conclusions or failed drug development efforts.

Clinical research particularly depends on accurate measurements for patient care and treatment efficacy assessment. Precise measurements of vital signs, drug dosages, and biological markers directly influence treatment decisions and patient outcomes. The standardization of these measurements across different healthcare settings ensures consistent patient care and reliable research data.

In ecological studies, measurement accuracy affects our understanding of population dynamics, biodiversity assessments, and environmental change impacts. Precise measurements of species abundance, habitat parameters, and environmental conditions enable researchers to track ecosystem changes and develop effective conservation strategies.

Pharmaceutical research relies heavily on measurement precision throughout the drug development pipeline. From initial compound screening to clinical trials, accurate measurements of drug concentrations, biological responses, and side effects determine drug safety and efficacy. Quality control in pharmaceutical manufacturing depends on precise analytical measurements to ensure product consistency and safety.

Genetic research requires exceptional measurement accuracy in DNA sequencing, gene expression analysis, and mutation detection. Modern genomic technologies can detect single nucleotide variations, making measurement precision crucial for understanding genetic diseases and developing targeted therapies.

Cell biology research depends on accurate measurements of cell populations, protein expression, and cellular responses. Flow cytometry, microscopy, and biochemical assays require precise calibration and standardization to generate reliable data about cellular processes and responses to various treatments.

Environmental monitoring in life sciences demands accurate measurements of various parameters including temperature, pH, chemical concentrations, and atmospheric conditions. These measurements inform our understanding of climate change impacts on biological systems and guide environmental protection efforts.

Agricultural research relies on precise measurements of crop yields, soil conditions, and plant responses to various treatments. Accurate measurement of these parameters enables optimization of agricultural practices and development of more resilient crop varieties.

Neuroscience research requires precise measurements of neural activity, neurotransmitter levels, and behavioral responses. Advanced imaging techniques and electrophysiological measurements must maintain high accuracy to reliably map brain function and understand neurological disorders.

The integration of measurement accuracy with statistical analysis ensures research validity and reproducibility. Modern life sciences increasingly employ automated measurement systems and digital data collection, requiring regular calibration and validation to maintain measurement accuracy across different platforms and laboratories.

Aspect	Description	Examples	Impact on Research
Precision	Degree of exactness in measurement	• DNA concentration • Blood pressure readings • Cell counts	Affects reliability of findings
Accuracy	Closeness to true value	• Diagnostic tests • Gene expression levels • Population estimates	Determines validity of conclusions
Resolution	Smallest detectable difference	• Microscopy detail • Temperature changes • pH variations	Influences detection of effects
Range	Span of measurable values	• Concentration ranges • Time scales • Size measurements	Defines study scope
Sensitivity	Response to small changes	• Enzyme assays • Hormone levels • Growth rates	Affects detection of subtle effects
Specificity	Measurement of target only	• Antibody tests • Gene probes • Species identification	Determines measurement accuracy

4.2 Types of Measurement Scales

Measurement scales provide essential frameworks for quantifying observations in scientific research, each offering distinct capabilities for data analysis and interpretation. Nominal scales represent the most basic form of measurement, focusing purely on categorization without inherent order. These scales find extensive application in taxonomic classification, genetic variants identification, and tissue type categorization. While mathematically limited, nominal scales provide crucial organizational structure for biological classification systems.

4.2.1 Ordinal scales

Ordinal scales introduce ranking capabilities while maintaining potentially unequal intervals between categories. In medical research, these scales prove invaluable for assessing disease progression, patient recovery stages, and treatment response levels. Common applications include pain assessment scales, tumor staging systems, and behavioral rating scales. Ordinal data supports non-parametric statistical analyses, making it particularly useful in clinical studies where exact measurement intervals may be difficult to establish.

4.2.2 Interval scales

Interval scales represent a significant advancement by introducing equal intervals between measurement points, though lacking a true zero point. Temperature measurements in biological systems exemplify this scale, enabling precise monitoring of physiological processes and environmental conditions. These scales support sophisticated statistical analyses, including means, standard deviations, and parametric tests, crucial for quantitative research in life sciences.

4.2.3 Ratio scales

Ratio scales offer the highest level of measurement precision, incorporating all properties of previous scales while including a meaningful zero point. These scales prove essential in laboratory research, enabling precise measurements of concentration, mass, length, and time. The presence of a true zero point allows for meaningful ratio comparisons and supports comprehensive statistical analyses, including geometric means and coefficients of variation.

The choice of measurement scale significantly impacts data analysis possibilities and interpretation. Researchers must carefully consider scale properties when designing studies and selecting statistical methods. Understanding scale limitations helps prevent inappropriate statistical applications and ensures valid conclusions from research data.

Modern research increasingly combines multiple measurement scales within single studies, particularly in complex biological systems. This integration requires careful consideration of scale properties during data analysis and interpretation. Advances in measurement technology continue to enhance precision across all scale types, though proper scale selection remains crucial for research validity.

4.2.4 Scale transformation and conversion

Scale transformation and conversion must be handled carefully to maintain data integrity. While some transformations between scales are possible, others may compromise data quality or introduce bias. Researchers must consider these limitations when designing studies and analyzing results.

Quality control measures differ across measurement scales, requiring specific validation approaches for each type. Reliability and validity assessments must account for scale properties, ensuring appropriate evaluation methods for different measurement types.

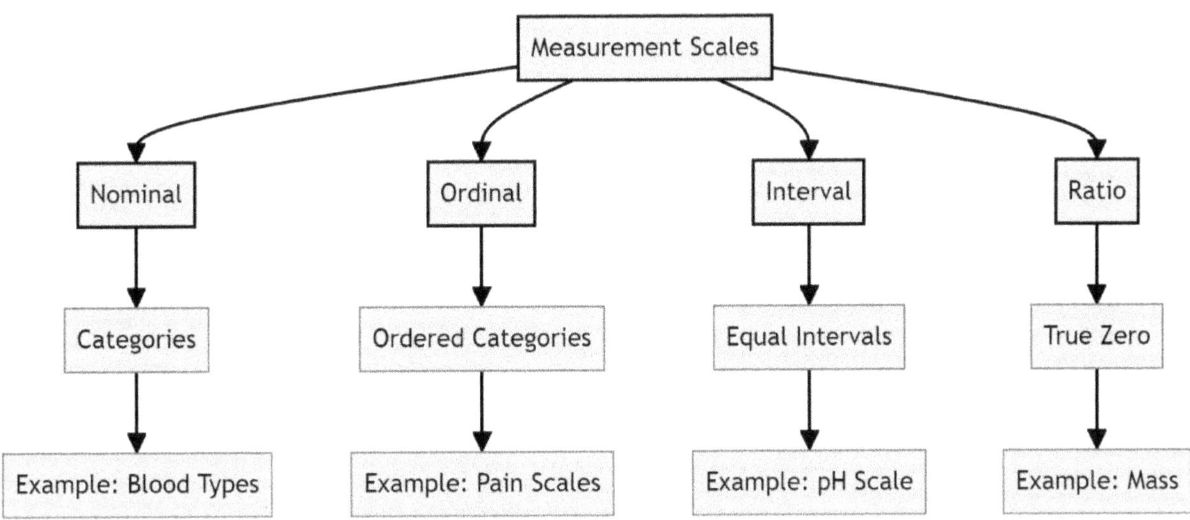

Fig. 4.2. Measurement Scales Hierarchy

4.3 Variables and Measurement Approaches

Variables in research represent characteristics or attributes that can be measured and often vary among subjects or conditions. These measurements must be approached with careful consideration of variable type, measurement scale, and intended analysis methods.

4.3.1 Independent variables

Independent variables, manipulated by researchers to study their effects, require precise control and documentation of manipulation methods. This includes maintaining consistent experimental conditions, recording intervention timing, and documenting any deviations from protocols. Proper measurement approaches for independent variables often involve standardized procedures and calibrated instruments to ensure reproducibility.

4.3.2 Dependent variables

Dependent variables, which respond to independent variable manipulation, demand careful selection of measurement tools and methods appropriate to the variable type. Continuous variables require instruments capable of precise measurement at appropriate scales, while categorical variables need clear classification criteria. Measurement approaches must account for potential confounding factors and measurement error.

4.3.3 Intervening variables

Intervening variables, which mediate between independent and dependent variables, often require complex measurement approaches combining multiple methods. These might include direct measurements, observational data, and validated assessment tools to capture the full complexity of the intervening process.

4.3.4 Confounding variables

Confounding variables necessitate careful measurement to control their effects on research outcomes. This includes implementing appropriate controls, randomization procedures, and statistical adjustments to account for their influence. Measurement approaches must be sensitive enough to detect and quantify confounding effects.

4.3.5 Categorical variables

Categorical variables require clear operational definitions and consistent classification criteria. This includes developing detailed coding schemes, training observers or raters, and establishing reliability measures for subjective classifications. Measurement approaches often involve standardized assessment tools or rubrics to ensure consistency.

4.3.6 Continuous variables

Continuous variables demand precision in measurement tools and procedures. This includes regular calibration of instruments, standardization of measurement conditions, and appropriate recording of measurement uncertainty. Measurement approaches must account for the full range of possible values and maintain consistent precision across that range.

4.3.7 Latent variables

Latent variables, not directly observable, require sophisticated measurement approaches often involving multiple indicators or proxy measures. This might include validated assessment scales, behavioral observations, or physiological measurements that collectively capture the underlying construct.

4.3.8 Time-dependent variables

Time-dependent variable present unique measurement challenges requiring careful consideration of temporal aspects. This includes determining appropriate measurement intervals, accounting for circadian rhythms or seasonal variations, and maintaining consistent timing across measurements.

Characteristics of Selected Variables			
Independent	**Dependent**	**Control**	**Extraneous**
Manipulated by researcher	Measured outcomes	Held constant	Potential confounders
Require precise control	Require sensitive detection	Require standardization	Require monitoring
Examples: Drug dosage, Temperature, Exercise intensity	Examples: Gene expression levels, Growth rates, Survival rates	Examples: Age, Gender, Environmental conditions	Examples: Diet, Stress levels, Time of day

Quality control in variable measurement involves regular validation of instruments, standardization of procedures, and monitoring of measurement consistency. This includes implementing appropriate quality assurance protocols, conducting reliability assessments, and maintaining detailed documentation of measurement procedures.

Variable Measurement Approaches			
Variable Type	**Measurement Considerations**	**Example Methods**	**Quality Control**
Continuous	• Precision requirements • Calibration needs • Range limitations	• Digital instruments • Analog scales • Automated systems	• Regular calibration • Multiple readings • Standard curves
Discrete	• Classification accuracy • Category definitions • Counting protocols	• Manual counts • Automated counters • Image analysis	• Double checking • Independent verification • Control samples
Categorical	• Clear definitions • Classification criteria • Observer training	• Visual inspection • Diagnostic tests • Scoring systems	• Inter-rater reliability • Standard references • Quality checks
Ordinal	• Scale validation • Rater training • Consistency checks	• Rating scales • Ranking systems • Grading schemes	• Standardization • Multiple raters • Reference standards

4.4 Ensuring Measurement Reliability and Validity

Measurement reliability and validity form the foundation of credible research in scientific endeavors. Reliability refers to the consistency of measurements across time, observers, and conditions, while validity ensures measurements accurately represent the intended constructs or phenomena under study.

4.4.1 Test-retest reliability

Test-retest reliability examines measurement consistency over time, requiring repeated measurements under identical conditions. This approach proves crucial in longitudinal studies and clinical trials where temporal stability of measurements impacts research conclusions. Researchers must carefully consider appropriate time intervals between measurements and control for potential learning effects or temporal variations.

4.4.2 Inter-rater reliability

Inter-rater reliability focuses on consistency across different observers or measurement operators. This becomes particularly critical in observational studies, behavioral assessments, and qualitative data coding. Training protocols, standardized rubrics, and regular calibration sessions help maintain consistency among multiple observers.

4.4.3 Internal consistency reliability

Internal consistency reliability evaluates the coherence of multiple items measuring the same construct. This proves essential in scale development and composite measurements, often assessed through statistical methods like Cronbach's alpha. Regular evaluation of internal consistency helps identify problematic items or measurement approaches requiring refinement.

4.4.4 Validity

Validity represents the accuracy of measurements in capturing the intended construct. **Content validity** ensures measurements comprehensively capture all relevant aspects of the studied phenomenon. This involves systematic review of measurement tools by subject matter experts, comprehensive literature reviews, and pilot testing to identify potential gaps or irrelevant components.

A. Construct validity examines whether measurements accurately reflect theoretical constructs. This includes convergent validity (correlation with related measures) and discriminant validity (distinction from unrelated constructs). Validation studies often employ multiple measurement approaches to establish construct validity.

B. Criterion validity relates measurements to established standards or outcomes. Predictive validity examines relationships with future outcomes, while concurrent validity compares measurements with existing validated tools. These assessments help establish practical utility and accuracy of measurements.

Measurement error analysis plays crucial role in reliability and validity assessment. Systematic errors require identification and correction through calibration procedures, while random errors necessitate appropriate statistical handling and measurement repetition.

Quality control procedures support reliability and validity through standardized protocols, regular instrument calibration, and operator training. Documentation of quality control measures, including calibration records and training logs, provides evidence of measurement quality.

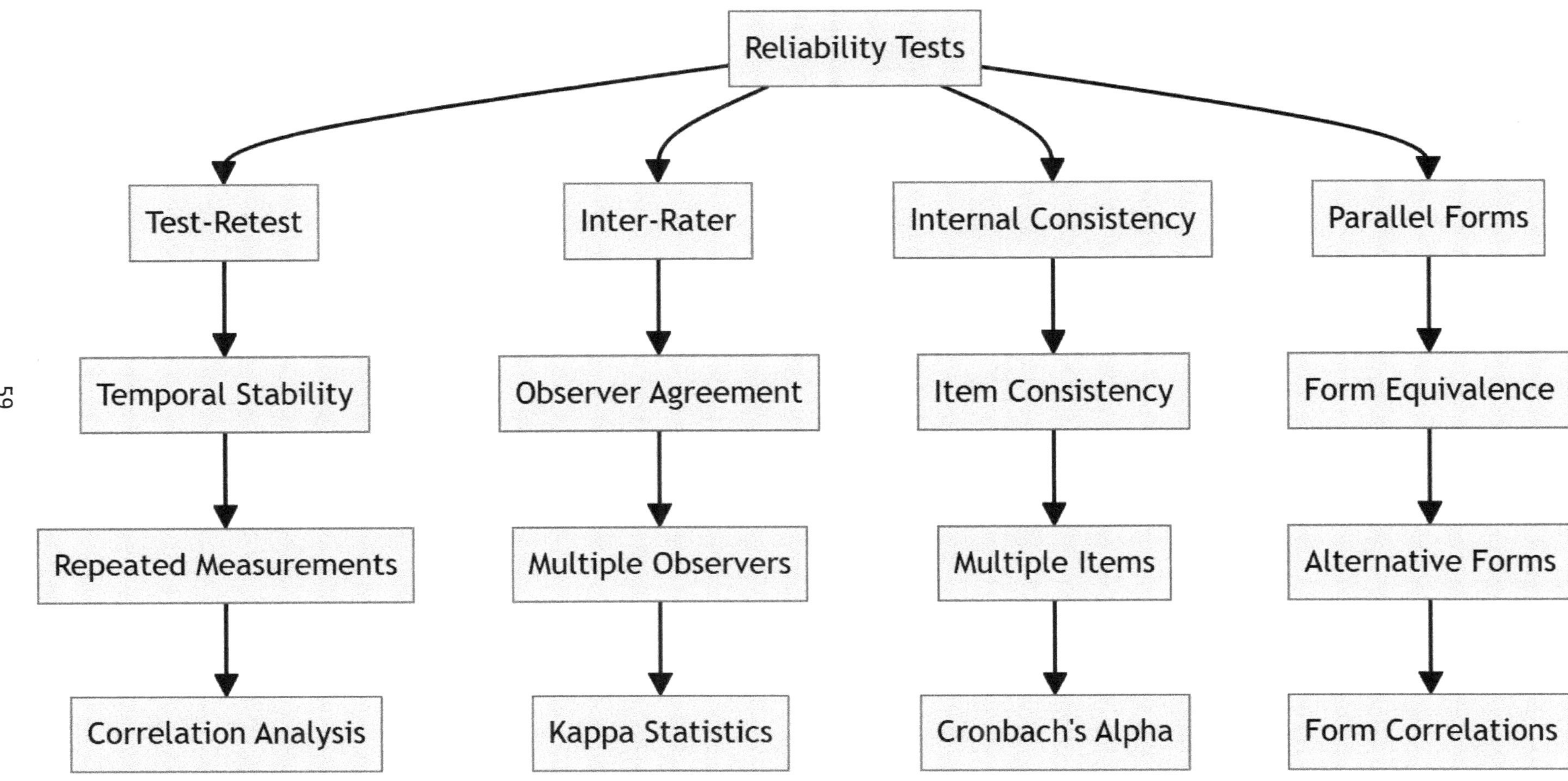

Fig. 4.3. Types of Reliability in Research Measurement

Statistical approaches to reliability and validity assessment include correlation analyses, factor analysis, and variance component analysis. These methods provide quantitative evidence of measurement quality while identifying areas requiring improvement.

4.5 Techniques for Improving Measurement Quality

Standardization of measurement procedures represents a fundamental technique for improving measurement quality. This includes developing detailed protocols for instrument calibration, sample preparation, and data collection procedures. Standard operating procedures (SOPs) should document every step of the measurement process, ensuring consistency across different operators and time periods.

Different types of validity must be considered:

Comprehensive Validity Framework			
Validity Type	**Definition**	**Assessment Methods**	**Examples in Life Sciences**
Content Validity	Coverage of construct domain	• Expert review • Literature analysis • Comprehensive mapping	• Disease symptom checklist • Species identification key • Diagnostic criteria
Construct Validity	Measurement of theoretical construct	• Factor analysis • Convergent testing • Discriminant testing	• Stress hormone measures • Immune function tests • Cognitive assessments
Criterion Validity	Correlation with external standard	• Concurrent validation • Predictive validation • Gold standard comparison	• New diagnostic test validation • Biomarker verification • Growth prediction models
Face Validity	Apparent measurement appropriateness	• Expert opinion • User feedback • Logical analysis	• Physical examination protocols • Behavioral observation forms • Patient questionnaires

Regular instrument calibration plays a critical role in measurement quality. This involves routine checks against known standards, maintenance schedules, and documentation of calibration procedures. Advanced calibration techniques may include multiple-point calibration curves, internal standards, and cross-validation with different measurement methods.

Training programs for personnel ensure consistent application of measurement techniques. This includes initial training, regular refresher sessions, and competency assessments. Documentation of training records and periodic evaluation of operator performance help maintain measurement quality.

Environmental control measures minimize external influences on measurements. This includes monitoring and controlling temperature, humidity, vibration, and electromagnetic interference. Purpose-built facilities with controlled conditions may be necessary for particularly sensitive measurements.

Quality control samples provide ongoing verification of measurement accuracy. These include blank samples, known standards, and control materials analyzed alongside research samples. Statistical process control charts help monitor measurement system performance over time.

Replicate measurements help quantify measurement precision and identify outliers. This includes technical replicates (repeated measurements of the same sample) and biological replicates (measurements of independent samples). Statistical analysis of replicates helps establish confidence intervals and measurement uncertainty.

Method validation studies ensure measurement techniques are fit for purpose. This includes evaluating linearity, precision, accuracy, detection limits, and measurement range. Validation protocols should follow established guidelines and regulatory requirements where applicable.

Data quality assessment procedures help identify measurement issues. This includes automated data checking algorithms, outlier detection methods, and trend analysis. Regular review of quality metrics helps maintain measurement system performance.

Documentation systems track all aspects of measurement processes. This includes instrument maintenance records, calibration certificates, training records, and raw data. Electronic laboratory information management systems (LIMS) can automate documentation and provide audit trails.

Proficiency testing through participation in inter-laboratory comparison programs helps verify measurement quality. These programs provide external assessment of measurement accuracy and highlight areas requiring improvement.

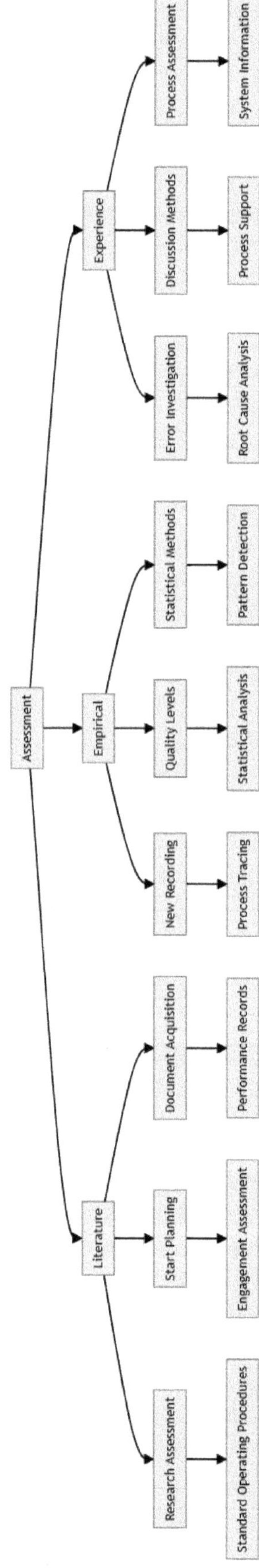

Fig. 4.4. Quality Control in Research Measurement

4.6 Practical Strategies for Maintaining Measurement Quality

Regular equipment maintenance and calibration schedules represent foundational strategies for maintaining measurement quality. This includes daily checks of basic functionality, weekly calibration procedures, and monthly comprehensive maintenance reviews. Documentation of all maintenance activities ensures traceability and identifies potential systematic issues early.

Standard operating procedures must be regularly updated and accessible to all personnel. These should include step-by-step protocols, troubleshooting guides, and quality control checkpoints. Regular review and revision of procedures incorporate new best practices and technological advances while maintaining measurement consistency.

Training programs require structured implementation with clear competency assessments. Initial training should cover theoretical foundations, practical demonstrations, and supervised practice sessions. Ongoing assessment through proficiency testing and periodic retraining maintains operator competency.

Environmental monitoring systems track conditions affecting measurement quality. Automated systems can continuously record temperature, humidity, and other relevant parameters. Alert systems notify personnel when conditions deviate from acceptable ranges, allowing prompt corrective action.

Quality control charts provide visual tools for tracking measurement system performance. These include Levey-Jennings charts for monitoring control sample results and Shewhart charts for process control. Regular statistical analysis of these charts helps identify trends or shifts in measurement quality.

Sample handling protocols ensure measurement integrity throughout the analytical process. This includes proper storage conditions, chain of custody documentation, and appropriate sample preparation procedures. Regular audits of sample handling practices help maintain compliance with established protocols.

Data management systems must include robust quality assurance features. Automated data validation checks can flag potential errors or outliers for review. Regular backup procedures and audit trails ensure data integrity and traceability.

Reference materials and standards require proper storage and handling. Certificate expiration dates must be tracked, and new standards obtained before expiration. Regular verification of standard quality ensures reliable calibration procedures.

Documentation systems should support easy retrieval and analysis of quality metrics. Electronic systems can automate data collection and generate regular quality reports. Trend analysis of these metrics helps identify areas requiring improvement.

Continuous improvement programs encourage regular evaluation and refinement of measurement processes. This includes regular review of quality metrics, incorporation of user feedback, and implementation of corrective actions when needed.

The integration of reliability and validity considerations throughout the research process ensures the scientific value and practical utility of research findings. Regular assessment and monitoring of these aspects helps maintain high standards of research quality and credibility in life sciences research.

5. Biostatistical Foundation

What is research but a blind date with knowledge?

-   Will Harvey

Statistics serves as the cornerstone for converting raw data into meaningful scientific insights. In life sciences, biostatistics provides the tools necessary for understanding biological variation, testing hypotheses, and drawing reliable conclusions from research data.

5.1 Introduction to Biostatistics in Life Sciences

Biostatistics serves as a fundamental pillar in life sciences research, providing the methodological foundation for designing studies, analyzing data, and drawing valid conclusions. This specialized branch of statistics adapts mathematical and statistical principles to address the unique challenges and complexities inherent in biological systems and medical research.

5.1.1 Core Functions in Research Design

At the outset of any research project, biostatistical principles guide crucial decisions about study design and methodology. Sample size determination represents a critical early application, ensuring studies have adequate statistical power to detect meaningful effects while avoiding wasteful oversampling. This process requires careful consideration of expected effect sizes, population variability, and desired confidence levels. Through power analysis and sample size calculations, researchers can optimize resource allocation while maintaining scientific validity.

The design of experimental protocols benefits substantially from biostatistical input. This includes determining appropriate control groups, randomization procedures, and strategies for minimizing bias. Factorial designs, split-plot arrangements, and nested hierarchies emerge from statistical principles that maximize information gain while controlling for confounding variables. The selection of appropriate measurement scales and data collection methods similarly relies on statistical considerations to ensure valid and reliable results.

5.1.2 Data Analysis and Interpretation

In the realm of data analysis, biostatistics provides a structured approach to extracting meaningful information from complex biological data. Descriptive statistics offer initial insights through measures of central tendency and dispersion, helping researchers understand data distributions and identify potential patterns or anomalies. These fundamental analyses provide the foundation for more sophisticated statistical investigations.

Inferential statistics enable researchers to move beyond sample descriptions to make broader conclusions about populations. This includes hypothesis testing, confidence interval estimation, and various modeling approaches. The selection of appropriate statistical tests requires careful consideration of data types, distributional assumptions, and research objectives. Biostatisticians help navigate these choices while ensuring proper application and interpretation of statistical methods.

5.1.3 Quality Control and Validation

Biostatistics plays a crucial role in maintaining research quality through various validation and quality control procedures. This includes methods for identifying outliers, assessing data quality, and evaluating measurement reliability. Statistical process control techniques help monitor ongoing data collection, ensuring consistency and identifying potential problems early in the research process.

The validation of analytical methods relies heavily on statistical approaches. This includes assessing method accuracy, precision, and reliability through various statistical measures. Biostatistical techniques help establish acceptable ranges for quality control parameters while providing frameworks for method comparison and standardization.

5.1.4 Integration with Modern Research Tools

Modern biostatistics increasingly integrates with computational tools and big data approaches. Statistical software packages provide powerful platforms for implementing complex analyses, while programming languages like R and Python offer flexibility for custom analytical solutions. Understanding these tools' statistical foundations remains crucial for proper application and interpretation.

Machine learning and artificial intelligence applications in life sciences research rely fundamentally on statistical principles. Biostatisticians help bridge traditional statistical approaches with modern computational methods, ensuring proper validation and interpretation of results from these advanced analytical tools.

5.1.5 Communication of Results

Effective communication of statistical results represents another crucial aspect of biostatistics in research. This includes appropriate presentation of numerical results, creation of informative visualizations, and clear explanation of statistical concepts to diverse audiences. Biostatisticians help ensure that statistical findings are presented accurately and comprehensibly while maintaining scientific rigor.

The interpretation of statistical significance requires careful consideration of both statistical and practical importance. Biostatisticians help researchers navigate these distinctions while considering effect sizes, confidence intervals, and other measures that provide context for statistical findings.

5.1.6 Evolving Role in Modern Research

The role of biostatistics continues to evolve with advancing research methodologies and technologies. New analytical challenges emerge from high-throughput technologies, longitudinal studies, and complex experimental designs. Biostatisticians help develop and adapt methodological approaches to address these challenges while maintaining scientific validity.

The integration of multiple data types and sources presents particular challenges in modern research. Biostatistical methods for data integration, meta-analysis, and systematic review help researchers synthesize evidence from various sources while accounting for different study designs and quality levels.

Success in applying biostatistics to life sciences research requires ongoing collaboration between researchers and statistical experts. This partnership ensures appropriate application of statistical methods while maintaining focus on meaningful biological questions. Through careful attention to biostatistical principles throughout the research process, investigators can enhance the quality and reliability of their scientific findings.

Understanding and properly applying biostatistical principles remains essential for conducting valid and reliable research in the life sciences. This foundation supports the advancement of scientific knowledge while maintaining methodological rigor and reliability in research findings.

5.2 Common Biostatistical Software Tools

The landscape of biostatistical software has evolved significantly, offering researchers powerful tools for data analysis and visualization. Understanding the capabilities, limitations, and appropriate applications of these tools is crucial for effective research implementation.

5.2.1 R Statistical Computing Environment

R represents one of the most versatile and widely-used platforms for biostatistical analysis. This open-source software provides exceptional flexibility through its extensive package ecosystem, particularly suited for life sciences research. The Bioconductor project, specifically designed for biological data analysis, offers specialized packages for genomics, proteomics, and other high-throughput biological data.

R's strengths include its comprehensive statistical capabilities, from basic descriptive statistics to advanced modeling techniques. The software excels in producing publication-quality graphics and supports reproducible research through R Markdown documents. However, its command-line interface presents a steeper learning curve compared to point-and-click software options. Users must invest time in learning R programming concepts and syntax.

Users benefit from R's active community support, extensive documentation, and regular updates. The software's ability to handle large datasets and integrate with other tools makes it particularly valuable for modern biomedical research. Additionally, R's open-source nature ensures transparency in statistical methods and promotes method sharing within the scientific community.

5.2.2 SPSS (Statistical Package for Social Sciences)

SPSS, while originally developed for social sciences, has found widespread application in biomedical research. Its intuitive graphical user interface makes it particularly accessible for researchers without extensive programming experience. The software provides comprehensive statistical capabilities through menu-driven options, making it suitable for standard biostatistical analyses.

The strength of SPSS lies in its user-friendly approach to data management and analysis. Its point-and-click interface allows researchers to perform complex analyses without writing code. The software excels in handling survey data and performing standard statistical tests commonly used in clinical research. However, SPSS's commercial nature means significant licensing costs, and its flexibility for customization is more limited compared to programming-based alternatives.

5.2.3 SAS (Statistical Analysis System)

SAS represents an industry standard in clinical research and pharmaceutical development. Its comprehensive suite of tools provides robust capabilities for complex statistical analyses, particularly in clinical trials and regulated research environments. The software offers excellent data handling capabilities and supports processing of large datasets.

SAS programming requires specific syntax knowledge but provides powerful tools for data manipulation and analysis. The software's strength lies in its ability to handle complex study designs and provide validated output suitable for regulatory submissions. However, high licensing costs and a steep learning curve may present barriers for smaller research groups or individual investigators.

5.2.4 GraphPad Prism

GraphPad Prism has gained popularity in life sciences research for its focus on scientific graphing and biostatistical analysis. The software combines intuitive data entry with powerful visualization capabilities, making it particularly suitable for experimental research data. Its built-in statistical tests cover most common analyses needed in laboratory research.

Biostatistical Software Comparison				
Software	Primary Use Cases	Advantages	Limitations	Best For
R	• Advanced statistical analysis • Custom programming • Data visualization	• Free and open-source • Extensive packages • Flexible	• Steep learning curve • Command-line interface • Memory limitations	Researchers needing customization
SPSS	• Basic to intermediate stats • Survey analysis • Clinical trials	• User-friendly interface • Comprehensive tools • Good documentation	• Expensive • Limited flexibility • Resource intensive	Clinical researchers
SAS	• Large dataset analysis • Clinical trials • Regulatory compliance	• Industry standard • Powerful tools • Excellent support	• Very expensive • Complex syntax • Resource heavy	Pharmaceutical research
GraphPad Prism	• Basic statistics • Scientific graphing • Life science focus	• Intuitive interface • Publication-ready graphs • Built for life sciences	• Limited advanced stats • Expensive • Platform dependent	Lab-based researchers

Prism's strength lies in its ability to produce publication-quality graphs easily while providing integrated statistical analysis. The software includes extensive guidance on choosing appropriate statistical tests and interpreting results. However, its capabilities for handling large datasets or performing advanced statistical modeling are more limited compared to comprehensive statistical packages.

5.2.5 Python with Statistical Libraries

Python, while not primarily a statistical software, has emerged as a powerful tool for biostatistical analysis through libraries like NumPy, Pandas, and SciPy. These tools provide flexible options for data manipulation and statistical analysis while integrating with Python's broader capabilities in scientific computing and machine learning.

The combination of Python's statistical libraries with tools like Jupyter notebooks enables reproducible research and clear documentation of analytical procedures. However, like R, Python requires programming knowledge and presents a learning curve for researchers without coding experience.

5.2.6 Stata

Stata provides a balanced approach between programming flexibility and user-friendly interface. The software excels in handling longitudinal data and complex survey designs, making it particularly useful for epidemiological research and clinical studies. Its command syntax is more intuitive than some alternatives while maintaining powerful analytical capabilities.

5.2.7 Selection Considerations

Choosing appropriate biostatistical software requires consideration of several factors:

- Research needs and complexity of analyses required

- Data size and type

- User expertise and learning curve considerations

- Budget constraints and licensing costs

- Requirements for regulatory compliance

- Need for reproducibility and transparency

- Integration with other research tools

Success in implementing biostatistical software tools requires:

- Adequate training and support resources

- Regular updates and maintenance

- Quality control procedures for analysis

- Documentation of analytical procedures

- Validation of results across platforms when appropriate

Through careful selection and implementation of appropriate biostatistical software tools, researchers can enhance their analytical capabilities while maintaining efficiency and reliability in their statistical analyses. Regular evaluation of emerging tools and updates helps ensure continued effectiveness of biostatistical analyses in research applications.

5.3 Descriptive Statistics

Descriptive statistics provide fundamental tools for summarizing and understanding data characteristics in biomedical research. These methods help researchers identify patterns, describe distributions, and communicate data features effectively through both numerical summaries and visual representations.

5.3.1 Measures of Central Tendency

The mean, median, and mode represent the primary measures of central tendency, each providing unique insights into data distribution characteristics.

The arithmetic mean serves as the most commonly used measure of central tendency, calculated by summing all values and dividing by the number of observations. While mathematically straightforward, the mean's sensitivity to extreme values requires careful consideration in biomedical research. In skewed distributions or when outliers are present, the mean may not accurately represent the typical value. For instance, in studies of hospital length of stay, a few extremely long stays can substantially inflate the mean, potentially misleading interpretation of typical patient experiences.

The median, representing the middle value when data are arranged in order, provides a robust alternative to the mean. Being less sensitive to extreme values, the median often better represents central tendency in skewed distributions. This makes it particularly valuable in biological data, which frequently display asymmetrical distributions. For example, in measuring drug concentration levels in blood, the median might better represent typical values when some patients show unusually high absorption rates.

The mode, identifying the most frequently occurring value, has particular utility with categorical data or discrete numerical values. In genetic studies, for instance, the mode might identify the most common allele in a population. Multiple modes can provide insight into potential subgroups within data distributions.

Measures of Central Tendency		
Mean (Arithmetic Average)	**Median**	**Mode**
• Calculation: $\Sigma x/n$	• Middle value when ordered	• Most frequent value
• Best for: Normally distributed data	• Best for: Skewed distributions	• Best for: Categorical data
• Sensitive to outliers	• Robust to outliers	• Can be multiple modes
• Example: Average blood glucose levels	• Example: Survival times	• Example: Most common blood type

5.3.2 Measures of Dispersion

Dispersion measures quantify data spread, providing crucial information about variability and distribution characteristics.

The **range**, calculated as the difference between maximum and minimum values, offers a simple measure of data spread. While easily understood, its dependence on only two extreme values makes it sensitive to outliers. In biological systems, where extreme values might represent measurement errors or genuine but rare phenomena, the range requires careful interpretation.

Variance represents the average squared deviation from the mean, providing a fundamental measure of variability. Its calculation involves summing squared differences between each value and the mean, then dividing by degrees of freedom (n-1 for sample variance). While mathematically important, variance's squared units can complicate interpretation in practical contexts.

The **standard deviation**, calculated as the square root of variance, returns to original measurement units and thus provides more interpretable measures of spread. In normally distributed data, approximately 68% of observations fall within one standard deviation of the mean, offering a practical framework for understanding variability. This becomes particularly useful in clinical research, where establishing normal ranges often relies on standard deviation-based criteria.

The **interquartile range** (IQR), measuring the spread between the 25th and 75th percentiles, provides another robust measure of dispersion. Less sensitive to outliers than standard deviation, IQR particularly suits skewed distributions common in biological data. Box plots utilizing IQR effectively visualize data distribution while identifying potential outliers.

5.3.3 Applications in Biomedical Research

Clinical trials often employ both central tendency and dispersion measures to characterize treatment effects. The mean difference between treatment groups, accompanied by standard deviations, helps quantify intervention impacts. However, when data show marked skewness, median and IQR might better represent group differences.

Laboratory research frequently encounters replicate measurements where understanding variability proves crucial. Coefficient of variation (CV), calculated as standard deviation divided by mean and expressed as percentage, provides standardized comparison of variability across different measurement scales or methods.

Population studies might employ all measures to fully characterize distributions. For instance, describing blood pressure in a population might include:

- Mean and standard deviation for overall distribution

- Median and IQR if distribution shows skewness

- Mode to identify common values

- Range to understand extreme values

Interpretation Considerations

Choice of appropriate descriptive statistics requires careful consideration of:

- Data distribution characteristics

- Presence of outliers

- Measurement scale properties

- Research question context

- Communication objectives

Sample size influences reliability of descriptive statistics. Larger samples generally provide more stable estimates of both central tendency and dispersion measures. Small samples require particular caution in interpretation and may benefit from reporting multiple measures.

Visual Representation

Effective presentation of descriptive statistics often combines numerical summaries with visual representations:

- Histograms showing distribution shape

- Box plots displaying median, quartiles, and outliers

- Scatter plots revealing patterns and relationships

- Error bars indicating variability measures

Through careful selection and interpretation of descriptive statistics, researchers can effectively summarize data characteristics while avoiding potential misrepresentation. Understanding both strengths and limitations of different measures ensures appropriate application in research contexts.

Success in applying descriptive statistics requires:

- Appropriate measure selection for data type

- Careful consideration of distribution characteristics

- Clear presentation of results

- Thoughtful interpretation within research context

- Integration with inferential statistical approaches

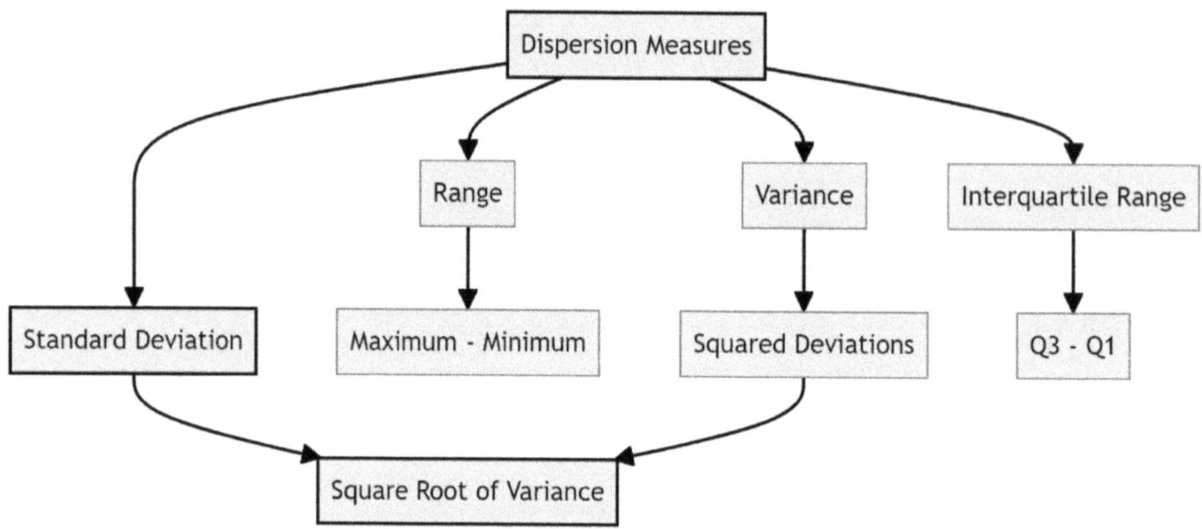

Fig. 5.1. Measures of Dispersion Relationships

5.4 Data Visualization Techniques

Data visualization serves as an essential tool in scientific research, transforming complex numerical data into comprehensible visual representations that reveal patterns, relationships, and trends that might otherwise remain obscured in raw data. The selection of appropriate visualization techniques depends on data type, research objectives, and intended audience, with each method offering unique advantages for specific applications.

5.4.1 Histograms

Histograms represent one of the most fundamental visualization tools, particularly valuable for displaying the distribution of continuous data. These graphs divide data into bins and display the frequency or proportion of observations within each interval, providing immediate visual insight into data distribution characteristics. Through histograms, researchers can readily assess distribution shape, identify potential outliers, and evaluate data spread patterns. The effectiveness of histograms relies heavily on appropriate bin width selection and clear axis labeling, with color usage becoming particularly important when comparing multiple distributions.

5.4.2 Box plots

Box plots, also known as box-and-whisker plots, offer a comprehensive view of data distribution characteristics through a single, efficient visualization. These plots display the median, interquartile range, and potential outliers, making them particularly valuable for comparing distributions across different groups or conditions. The box portion represents the interquartile range containing the middle 50% of the data, while the whiskers typically extend to 1.5 times the interquartile range, with individual points marking outliers beyond these boundaries. This visualization technique excels in providing quick comparisons of central tendency, spread, and symmetry across multiple groups.

5.4.3 Scatter plots

Scatter plots play a crucial role in visualizing relationships between two continuous variables, revealing correlation patterns, clustering tendencies, and potential outliers. These plots can be enhanced with regression lines, confidence intervals, and additional dimensional representations through color coding or point size variation. The versatility of scatter plots makes them invaluable for exploring relationships in complex datasets, particularly in studies examining associations between different variables or identifying patterns in experimental data.

5.4.4 Line graphs

Line graphs excel in displaying temporal trends or sequential measurements, making them particularly valuable in longitudinal studies or time-series analyses. These visualizations effectively communicate rates of change, cyclic variations, and comparative trends across different groups or conditions. In biomedical research, line graphs frequently appear in studies tracking physiological measurements over time, drug response curves, or population trend analyses. The clarity of trend visualization makes line graphs especially useful for communicating temporal patterns to diverse audiences.

5.4.5 Bar graphs

Bar graphs provide effective visualization for categorical data or discrete numerical comparisons, offering clear representations of quantities across different groups or categories. These graphs can be adapted through grouping or stacking to display more complex relationships, while error bars can be added to represent uncertainty or variability in measurements. The versatility of bar graphs makes them particularly valuable in communicating comparative data across different experimental conditions or treatment groups.

5.4.6 Pie diagrams

Pie diagrams, also known as pie charts, are a type of circular statistical graphic that is divided into proportional slices to illustrate numerical proportion. Pie charts are effective for displaying the relative sizes or proportions of different categories within a whole. They allow viewers to quickly grasp the composition of a dataset at a glance.

5.4.7 Heat maps

Heat maps offer sophisticated visualization for complex data matrices, using color intensity to represent value magnitude. This technique proves particularly valuable in genomics research for displaying gene expression patterns, correlation matrices, or other high-dimensional data sets. Effective heat map implementation requires careful attention to color scale selection and clear value-to-color mapping to ensure accurate data interpretation.

The implementation of visualization techniques requires careful consideration of design principles, technical accuracy, and communication effectiveness. Color selection must consider both aesthetic appeal and accessibility, including considerations for color-blind viewers. Scale selection and axis labeling demand particular attention to ensure accurate data representation while maintaining clear communication of research findings.

Success in data visualization relies heavily on appropriate software selection and quality control measures. Researchers must consider software capabilities, user expertise requirements, and output quality when selecting visualization tools. Regular quality control checks ensure accuracy and consistency in visual representations while maintaining scientific rigor in data presentation.

Through thoughtful selection and implementation of visualization techniques, researchers can effectively communicate complex scientific findings to diverse audiences while maintaining accuracy and accessibility. Regular evaluation of visualization effectiveness, combined with attention to design principles and technical requirements, ensures optimal communication of research results in scientific contexts.

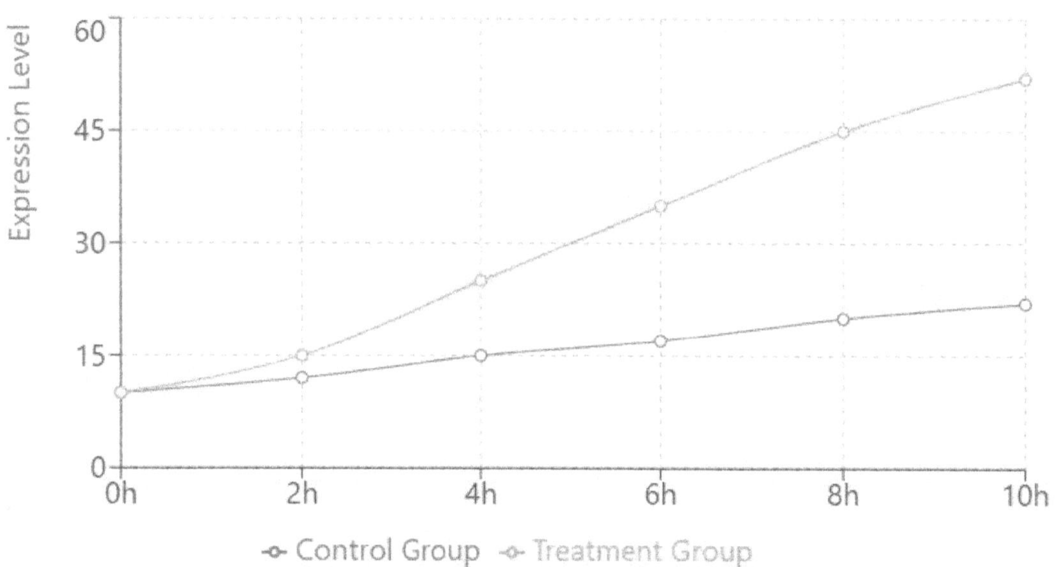

Fig. 5.2. Data Visualization Example

5.5 Inferential Statistics Basics

Inferential statistics represents a fundamental framework in scientific research, enabling researchers to draw conclusions about populations based on sample data. This branch of statistics moves beyond simple data description to provide tools for hypothesis testing, parameter estimation, and prediction, forming the backbone of evidence-based research conclusions.

The foundation of inferential statistics rests on probability theory and sampling distributions. Understanding these concepts is crucial as they provide the theoretical basis for making inferences about populations. The central limit theorem plays a pivotal role, stating that sampling distributions of means approach normal distribution as sample size increases, regardless of the underlying population distribution. This theorem provides the theoretical foundation for many statistical procedures used in research.

Hypothesis testing forms a core component of inferential statistics, providing a systematic approach to decision-making about research questions. The process begins with formulating **null** and **alternative hypotheses**, representing competing claims about population parameters. The null hypothesis typically represents no effect or no difference, while the alternative hypothesis suggests the presence of an effect or difference. This framework allows researchers to make probabilistic decisions about population characteristics based on sample evidence.

Statistical significance and **p-values** represent crucial concepts in hypothesis testing. The p-value quantifies the probability of obtaining results as extreme as those observed, assuming the null hypothesis is true. Conventional significance levels, typically set at 0.05 or 0.01, provide decision criteria for rejecting or failing to reject null hypotheses. However, modern statistical practice emphasizes the importance of considering effect sizes and confidence intervals alongside p-values for more comprehensive interpretation.

Confidence intervals provide a range of plausible values for population parameters, offering more information than point estimates alone. These intervals, typically constructed at 95% confidence level, help researchers understand the precision of their estimates while providing a measure of uncertainty. The width of confidence intervals relates to sample size and variability, with larger samples generally providing narrower, more precise intervals.

Parameter estimation represents another crucial aspect of inferential statistics. **Point estimates** provide single values for population parameters, while **interval estimates** offer ranges of plausible values. Maximum likelihood estimation and other statistical techniques help researchers obtain optimal estimates of population parameters from sample data. The precision of these estimates depends on sample size, measurement accuracy, and underlying population variability.

Type I and **Type II errors** require careful consideration in inferential statistics. Type I errors occur when researchers reject a true null hypothesis, while Type II errors involve failing to reject a false null hypothesis. The probability of

Type I error is controlled by the significance level (α), while Type II error probability (β) relates to statistical power. Understanding these error types helps researchers balance competing risks in their statistical decision-making.

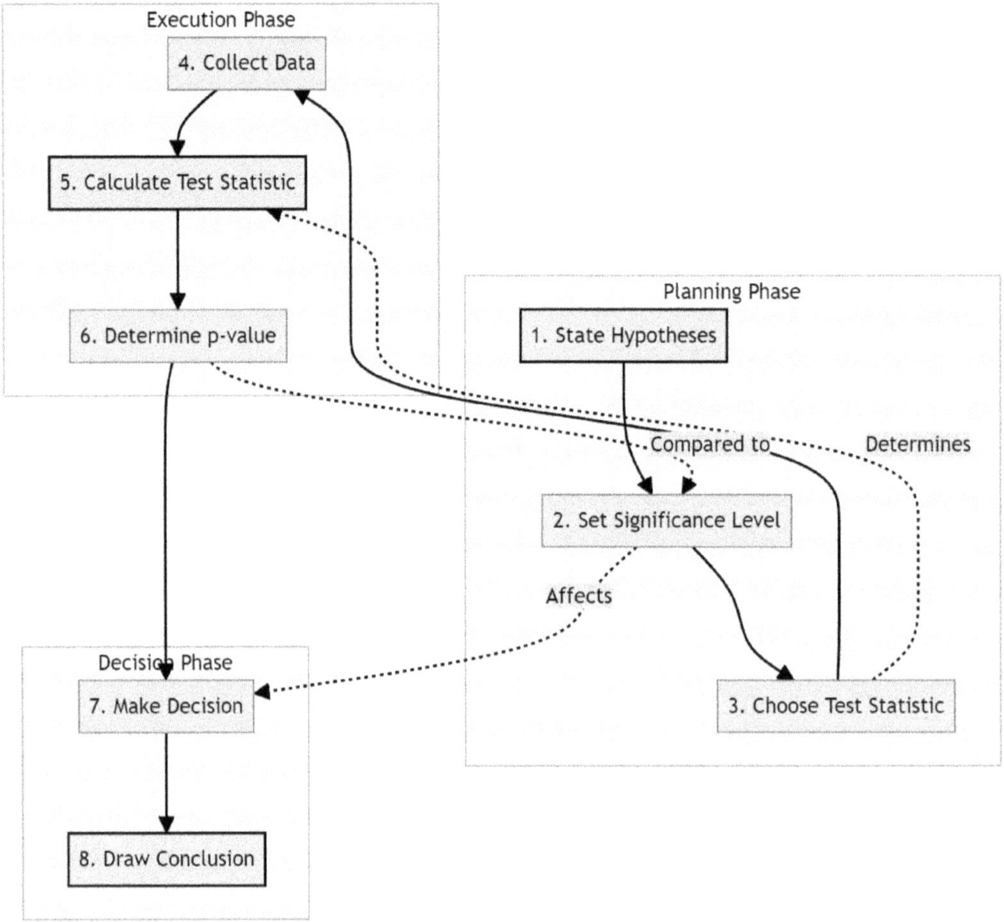

Fig. 5.3. Hypothesis Testing Process Flow

Statistical power, representing the probability of detecting true effects when they exist, plays a crucial role in research design. Power analysis helps determine appropriate sample sizes for studies, considering effect size, significance level, and desired power level. Adequate power ensures that studies can reliably detect meaningful effects while avoiding waste of resources on underpowered studies.

Assumptions underlying statistical tests demand careful attention in inferential statistics. Common assumptions include normality of distributions, independence of observations, and homogeneity of variances. Violation of these assumptions can affect test validity and reliability. Researchers must assess assumption validity and consider alternative approaches when assumptions are violated.

Non-parametric methods provide alternatives when parametric test assumptions are violated. These methods make fewer assumptions about underlying distributions and often use ranks rather than raw values. While generally less powerful than parametric tests under normal conditions, non-parametric methods offer robust alternatives for analyzing non-normal or ordinal data.

Effect size measures complement significance testing by quantifying the magnitude of relationships or differences. Common effect size measures include Cohen's d for mean differences and correlation coefficients for relationships. These measures help researchers assess practical significance alongside statistical significance, providing context for research findings.

The application of inferential statistics requires careful consideration of:

- Research design appropriateness
- Sample size adequacy
- Measurement reliability
- Statistical assumption validity
- Effect size interpretation
- Results generalizability

Success in applying inferential statistics depends on:

- Clear research questions
- Appropriate statistical method selection
- Careful assumption checking
- Thorough result interpretation
- Transparent reporting practices

Through careful application of inferential statistical principles, researchers can draw valid conclusions from sample data while maintaining appropriate recognition of uncertainty and limitations in their findings. This approach supports evidence-based decision-making while advancing scientific knowledge through rigorous statistical analysis.

5.6 Concept of Population and Sample

Population and sample concepts form the cornerstone of statistical inference in scientific research. The relationship between these elements provides the foundation for drawing meaningful conclusions about larger groups based on studying smaller, representative subsets.

A **population** represents the entire group about which information is desired and conclusions are to be drawn. In research contexts, populations can be finite or infinite, homogeneous or heterogeneous. For instance, in medical research, a population might comprise all patients with a specific condition, while in ecological studies, it might include all organisms of a particular species in a defined area. The complete enumeration of a population, known as a census, often proves impractical due to time, cost, and accessibility constraints.

Population parameters represent the true characteristics of interest in the entire population, such as means, proportions, or variances. These parameters usually remain unknown and must be estimated through sample statistics. Understanding population characteristics helps researchers design appropriate sampling strategies and determine suitable statistical approaches for analysis.

A **sample** constitutes a subset of the population selected for study purposes. The fundamental goal of sampling is to obtain a representative group that reflects the characteristics of the larger population. The relationship between sample and population critically influences the validity of research conclusions. Sample statistics serve as estimates of population parameters, with their accuracy depending largely on sampling method appropriateness and sample size adequacy.

5.7 Sampling Methods: Approaches to Selection

Probability Sampling methods rely on random selection principles, ensuring each population member has a known, non-zero probability of selection. Simple random sampling represents the most basic probability method, where each population member has an equal chance of selection. This method provides a foundation for statistical inference but may prove challenging to implement in large or geographically dispersed populations.

Systematic sampling involves selecting every nth member from a population list after a random start. While offering practical advantages in implementation, this method can introduce bias if the population contains underlying periodic patterns. Researchers must carefully consider population characteristics when employing systematic sampling to avoid systematic bias.

Stratified random sampling divides the population into subgroups (strata) based on relevant characteristics before random sampling within each stratum. This method ensures representation of important population subgroups and often provides more precise estimates than simple random sampling. Healthcare research frequently employs stratification by age, gender, or disease severity to ensure comprehensive population representation.

Cluster sampling selects groups rather than individuals, often employed when studying naturally occurring clusters like schools or communities. This approach can reduce sampling costs but may increase sampling error due to potential within-cluster homogeneity. Multi-stage cluster sampling extends this concept through multiple selection levels, balancing practical constraints with statistical precision.

Non-probability sampling methods, while not supporting formal statistical inference, serve important roles in specific research contexts. Convenience sampling selects readily available subjects, often used in pilot studies or preliminary research. Purposive sampling chooses subjects based on specific characteristics, particularly valuable in qualitative research or studying rare populations.

Quota sampling ensures representation of population subgroups through pre-established quotas, similar to stratified sampling but without random selection within quotas. This method helps maintain population proportion representation but may introduce selection bias through non-random selection processes.

A. Sample Size Considerations

Determining appropriate sample size involves balancing statistical precision requirements with practical constraints. Factors influencing sample size determination include:

- Desired precision level
- Population variability
- Confidence level requirements
- Expected effect size
- Available resources
- Study design characteristics

B. Sampling Error and Bias

Sampling error represents random variation between sample statistics and population parameters, naturally occurring in any sampling process. This error typically decreases with larger sample sizes, following the inverse square root relationship described by the central limit theorem.

Sampling bias introduces systematic differences between sample and population characteristics, potentially arising from:

- Inadequate sampling frame
- Non-response patterns
- Selection method flaws
- Coverage limitations

C. Implementation Considerations

Successful sampling implementation requires:

- Clear population definition

- Appropriate sampling frame development

- Suitable method selection

- Adequate sample size determination

- Quality control procedures

- Documentation of procedures

Through careful consideration of population characteristics and sampling method selection, researchers can obtain representative samples supporting valid statistical inference. Regular evaluation of sampling effectiveness helps maintain research quality while identifying potential improvements in sampling procedures.

5.8 Probability Distributions

Probability distributions are mathematical functions that describe the likelihood of different outcomes in a given situation. They are fundamental to statistical analysis and are used extensively in fields such as finance, engineering, and the natural sciences. Four key probability distributions are the normal distribution, t-distribution, chi-square distribution, and F-distribution.

5.8.1 Normal Distribution

The normal distribution, also known as the Gaussian distribution, is one of the most widely used probability distributions. It is a symmetric, bell-shaped curve that is defined by two parameters: the mean (μ) and the standard deviation (σ).

The normal distribution has the following properties:

- The curve is symmetric about the mean, μ.

- Approximately 68% of the data falls within 1 standard deviation (σ) of the mean.

- Approximately 95% of the data falls within 2 standard deviations of the mean.

- Approximately 99.7% of the data falls within 3 standard deviations of the mean.

The normal distribution is widely used in statistical analysis because many real-world phenomena, when aggregated, tend to follow a normal distribution. Examples include heights, weights, test scores, and measurement errors.

5.8.2 t-Distribution

The t-distribution, also known as Student's t-distribution, is a family of probability distributions that are similar to the normal distribution but have heavier tails. The t-distribution is used when the sample size is small and the population standard deviation is unknown.

The t-distribution has one parameter, the degrees of freedom (df), which determines the shape of the distribution. As the degrees of freedom increase, the t-distribution approaches the normal distribution.

The t-distribution is commonly used for:

- Constructing confidence intervals for small sample sizes
- Performing hypothesis testing when the population standard deviation is unknown
- Analyzing the statistical significance of regression coefficients

The t-distribution is particularly useful when working with small samples, as it provides a more accurate representation of the uncertainty in the data compared to the normal distribution.

5.8.3 Chi-Square Distribution

The chi-square (χ^2) distribution is a probability distribution used to model the sum of the squares of independent standard normal random variables. It is a right-skewed distribution with one parameter, the degrees of freedom (df), which determines the shape of the distribution.

The chi-square distribution is used in various statistical tests, including:

1. *Goodness-of-fit tests*: Evaluating how well a set of observed data fits a hypothesized distribution.
2. *Independence tests*: Determining whether two categorical variables are independent.

The chi-square distribution is particularly useful for hypothesis testing, as it allows researchers to quantify the probability of observing a particular test statistic under the null hypothesis.

5.8.4 F-Distribution

The F-distribution, named after the statistician Sir Ronald Fisher, is a continuous probability distribution used in the analysis of variance (ANOVA) and other statistical tests. The F-distribution is defined by two parameters: the numerator degrees of freedom (df1) and the denominator degrees of freedom (df2).

The F-distribution is used in the following statistical tests:

- **One-way ANOVA**: Comparing the means of three or more independent groups.

- **Two-way ANOVA**: Analyzing the effects of two independent variables on a dependent variable.

- **Multiple regression analysis**: Evaluating the overall significance of a regression model.

- **Variance ratio tests**: Comparing the variances of two independent samples.

The F-distribution is particularly useful for making inferences about the equality of variances in different populations, as well as for determining the statistical significance of the overall fit of a regression model.

5.9 Working with Biostatistical Data

The quality of statistical analysis depends heavily on the integrity and preparation of the underlying data. Working with biostatistical data requires systematic approaches to ensure accuracy and reliability.

A. Data Cleaning Process

Data cleaning, also known as data cleansing or data scrubbing, is a critical process in data management that ensures the quality, accuracy, and reliability of data before analysis. This systematic process involves identifying and correcting errors, inconsistencies, and inaccuracies in datasets to maintain data integrity and support reliable analytical outcomes.

Initial Data Assessment and Inspection: The process begins with a comprehensive review of the raw data to understand its structure, format, and content. This initial inspection involves examining data types, identifying missing values, and assessing the overall data architecture. Data profiling tools are often employed to generate summary statistics, frequency distributions, and pattern analysis, providing insights into potential data quality issues.

Quality Assessment: Following initial inspection, a thorough quality assessment is conducted to identify specific data issues. This phase focuses on detecting:

- Missing or incomplete data entries

- Duplicate records

- Inconsistent formatting or coding

- Outliers and anomalies

- Structural errors in data organization

- Data type mismatches

- Standardization needs

Data Cleaning Implementation: The actual cleaning process involves systematic correction of identified issues through various methods:

1. Missing Data Management

   - Deletion of records (when appropriate)

   - Statistical imputation

   - Default value assignment

   - Manual data entry for critical values

2. Standardization

   - Consistent formatting across similar data fields

   - Unit conversion standardization

   - Categorical data harmonization

   - Text case and format normalization

3. Error Correction

   - Fixing typographical errors

   - Resolving inconsistencies

   - Correcting invalid entries

   - Addressing structural issues

Validation and Quality: Control After implementing cleaning procedures, rigorous validation ensures the effectiveness of the cleaning process:

- Cross-referencing cleaned data against source data

- Verification of cleaning logic and rules

- Statistical validation of corrected values

- Consistency checks across related data fields

- Assessment of data completeness and accuracy

Documentation and Reporting: Comprehensive documentation is essential for maintaining transparency and reproducibility:

- Detailed logging of all cleaning procedures

- Documentation of decision rules and criteria

- Recording of changes made to the original dataset

- Maintenance of cleaning scripts and protocols

- Version control of datasets

Best Practices and Considerations: Several key principles guide effective data cleaning:

- Preserve original data by working with copies

- Implement automated cleaning processes where possible

- Maintain consistent cleaning protocols

- Regular validation throughout the cleaning process

- Clear documentation of all procedures

- Iterative approach to quality improvement

Impact and Importance: Proper data cleaning is fundamental to:

- Ensuring accurate analysis results

- Maintaining data integrity

- Supporting reliable decision-making

- Reducing analytical errors

- Improving operational efficiency

- Meeting regulatory compliance requirements

The data cleaning process requires a balanced approach between automation and manual intervention, with careful consideration of the specific context and requirements of the dataset. Success in data cleaning is measured not only by the removal of errors but also by the maintenance of data integrity and the support of subsequent analytical processes. Regular review and updates of cleaning procedures ensure continued effectiveness and adaptation to evolving data quality challenges.

B. Data Coding Standards

Data coding standards represent essential protocols in research methodology that ensure consistency, reliability, and interpretability of collected data. These standards provide a structured framework for converting raw information into standardized formats suitable for analysis while maintaining data integrity throughout the research process.

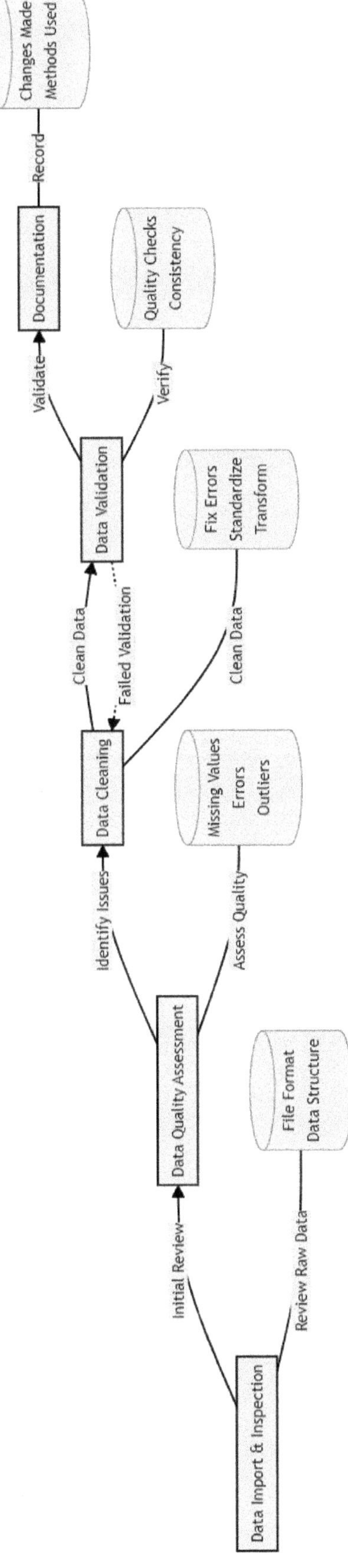

Fig. 5.4. Data Cleaning and Preparation Workflow

Fundamental Principles: Effective data coding standards incorporate several key principles. Variable naming conventions must be clear, consistent, and meaningful, avoiding special characters and spaces that could cause processing issues. Categorical variables require well-defined coding schemes that are mutually exclusive and exhaustive, while numeric variables need specified measurement units and precision levels. Missing data protocols should clearly distinguish between different types of missing values (e.g., not applicable, refused, unknown).

Implementation Guidelines: The implementation of coding standards requires systematic attention to detail. Documentation must include comprehensive codebooks that define all variables, their allowable values, and their relationships. Value labels should be descriptive yet concise, facilitating both data entry and analysis. Standard operating procedures should address data entry protocols, validation checks, and quality control measures.

Quality Assurance Measures: Regular quality checks ensure adherence to coding standards. These include automated validation rules to flag invalid entries, consistency checks across related variables, and periodic audits of coded data. Double-coding subsets of data by independent coders helps establish reliability metrics and identify potential systematic errors.

Best Practices: Several best practices enhance the effectiveness of coding standards:

- Establish clear documentation procedures

- Maintain version control of coding schemes

- Implement regular training for data entry personnel

- Conduct periodic reviews of coding efficiency

- Ensure compatibility with analysis software

- Create standardized error-checking protocols

Data coding standards fundamentally support research quality by ensuring data consistency and reliability. Their proper implementation facilitates efficient data processing, reduces errors, and enhances the reproducibility of research findings. Regular review and updates of coding standards ensure their continued relevance and effectiveness in meeting evolving research needs.

C. Data Integrity Checks

Ensuring data integrity is crucial for reliable analysis and decision-making. Key data integrity checks include:

1. *Range Checks*

- **Verify values are within plausible ranges**: Identify data points that fall outside expected bounds, which could indicate errors or outliers. This helps catch biologically/physically impossible values.

- **Flag potential outliers**: Detect extreme values that may warrant further investigation or exclusion from analysis.

2. *Consistency Checks*

- **Cross-reference related variables**: Validate that values across related data fields are logically consistent. For example, ensure birth year is earlier than current year.

- **Verify logical relationships**: Confirm that interdependent variables follow expected patterns. Spot impossible combinations that suggest data quality issues.

3. *Documentation and Metadata*:

- **Define variables clearly**: Provide unambiguous descriptions of what each data field represents.

- **Document units and measurement methods**: Ensure consistency and proper interpretation of values.

- **Capture data collection procedures**: Record how the data was gathered to assess potential biases or errors.

- **Note quality control measures**: Document steps taken to ensure data accuracy, such as cross-checks or verification processes.

- **Record analysis assumptions**: Outline any presumptions made when working with the data to aid proper interpretation of results.

Implementing these data integrity checks helps ensure the accuracy, reliability, and completeness of the data before analysis. This upfront work pays dividends by preventing downstream errors, improving analytical rigor, and supporting sound decision-making. Regular application of these checks throughout the data lifecycle is essential for maintaining data quality.

D. Best Practices for Data Management

Effective data management is essential for ensuring data quality, security, and accessibility. Key best practices include:

1. *Version Control*

- **Maintain data versions**: Keep track of changes to data over time by versioning datasets. This allows you to revert to previous states or investigate how the data has evolved.

- **Document modifications**: Record details about each version, such as when changes were made, what was updated, and who made the changes. This metadata helps understand the data's history.

- **Track changes**: Use version control systems, like Git, to efficiently manage and audit data revisions.

Data Coding and Management Standards			
Aspect	**Guidelines**	**Examples**	**Quality Control Measures**
Variable Naming	• Consistent format • Clear meaning • No spaces • Unique identifiers	• age_years • blood_glucose_mmol • treatment_group	• Naming convention document • Automated checks • Peer review
Value Coding	• Standardized codes • Clear documentation • Consistent format	• Sex: 1=M, 2=F • Status: 0=Negative, 1=Positive • Groups: A, B, C	• Codebook maintenance • Regular audits • Cross-validation
Missing Data	• Consistent codes • Type identification • Documentation	• NA = Not Available • NR = No Response • 999 = System Missing	• Missing pattern analysis • Documentation review • Impact assessment
Data Types	• Appropriate format • Consistent units • Clear categories	• Dates: YYYY-MM-DD • Measurements: SI units • Categories: Defined levels	• Format verification • Unit consistency checks • Category validation

2. Backup Procedures

- **Implement regular backups**: Regularly create full copies of data to protect against loss due to accidents, hardware failures, or other issues.

- **Store backups in multiple locations**: Keep backup data in both on-site and off-site storage to safeguard against localized disasters.

- **Ensure secure storage**: Use encryption, access controls, and other security measures to protect backup data from unauthorized access or tampering.

3. Access Control

- **Manage user permissions**: Establish clear rules about who can access, modify, or delete data. This helps prevent accidental or malicious changes.

- **Maintain data security**: Implement authentication, authorization, and auditing mechanisms to control and monitor access to sensitive information.

- **Create audit trails**: Log all data access and modification events to enable investigation of any suspicious activities.

4. *Quality Assurance*

- **Conduct regular audits**: Periodically review data for accuracy, completeness, and consistency. This helps identify and address quality issues.

- **Perform validation checks**: Implement automated checks to flag potential errors or anomalies in the data, such as out-of-range values or missing fields.

- **Log and address errors**: Keep a record of any data quality problems encountered, along with the steps taken to resolve them. This information can inform future improvements.

By consistently applying these best practices, we can ensure the integrity, security, and reliability of data assets. Properly managing data throughout its lifecycle helps support data-driven decision-making, regulatory compliance, and business continuity.

This page is intentionally left blank.

6. Hypothesis Testing

In research, an ounce of evidence is worth a pound of hypotheses.

-   Peter Medawar

Hypothesis testing forms the cornerstone of scientific inquiry, providing a systematic framework for evaluating research questions and drawing conclusions from data. In life sciences, this process is crucial for advancing our understanding of biological phenomena and validating scientific discoveries.

6.1 Basics of Hypothesis Formulation

The formulation of clear, testable hypotheses is fundamental to scientific research. A well-constructed hypothesis provides direction for study design and analysis while ensuring scientific rigor.

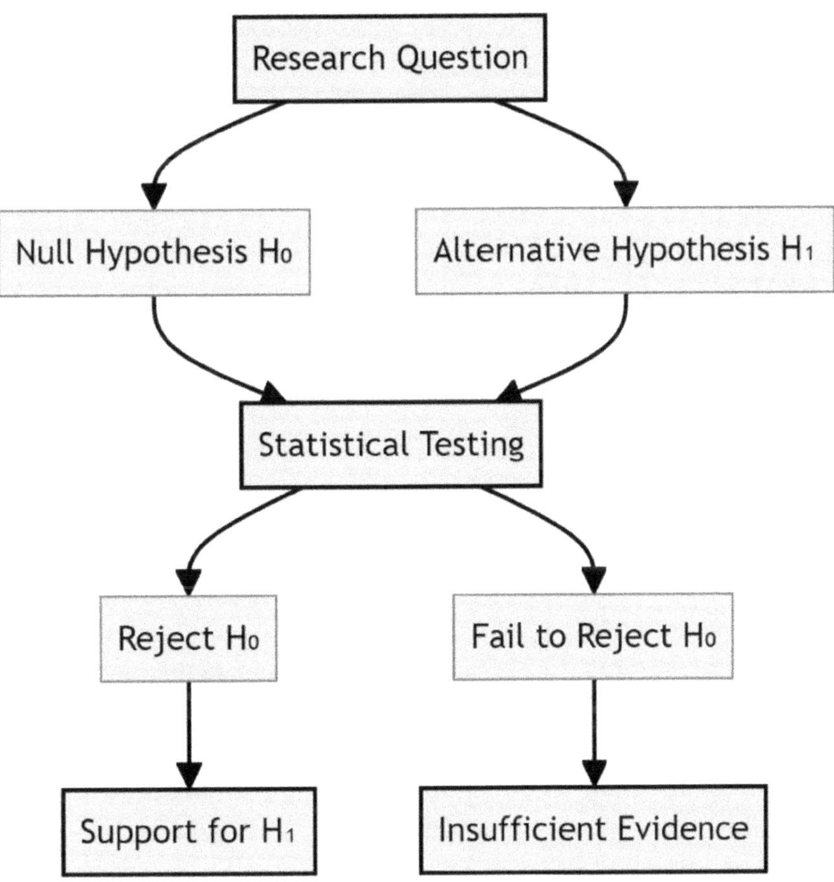

Fig. 6.1. Hypothesis Structure and Relationships

Common Research Scenarios and Hypothesis Formulation				
Research Context	**Null Hypothesis (H$_0$)**	**Alternative Hypothesis (H$_1$)**	**Example Variables**	**Typical Test**
Drug Efficacy	No difference between treatment and control	Treatment differs from control	Blood pressure reduction	t-test
Gene Expression	No difference in expression levels	Expression levels differ	mRNA levels	ANOVA
Disease Association	No association between factors	Factors are associated	Disease presence/absence	Chi-square
Survival Analysis	No difference in survival rates	Survival rates differ	Time to event	Log-rank test
Dose Response	No relationship between dose and response	Dose affects response	Enzyme activity	Regression
Population Comparison	No difference between populations	Populations differ	Species abundance	Mann-Whitney U
Time Series	No change over time	Change occurs over time	Growth rates	Repeated measures ANOVA
Correlation Study	No correlation between variables	Variables are correlated	Height/weight relationship	Pearson/Spearman

6.2 Steps in Hypothesis Testing

The hypothesis testing process follows a systematic sequence of steps to ensure reliable conclusions.

6.2.1 P-values and Significance Levels

P-values are fundamental statistical tools that help researchers quantify the strength of evidence against a null hypothesis. They represent the probability of obtaining test results at least as extreme as the observed results, assuming that the null hypothesis is true. Understanding p-values and significance levels is crucial for making informed decisions in statistical analysis.

Definition and Interpretation

A p-value is essentially a probability measure ranging from 0 to 1 that indicates the likelihood of obtaining observed results if the null hypothesis is true. Smaller p-values suggest stronger evidence against the null hypothesis, while larger p-values indicate weaker evidence. However, p-values do not measure the probability that the hypothesis is true or false, nor do they indicate the size or importance of an observed effect.

Common Significance Levels (α)

1. $\alpha = 0.05$ (**5% Level**)

- Most commonly used significance level

- 5% chance of Type I error (false positive)

- Considered a reasonable balance between Type I and Type II errors

- Standard in many fields of research

- 95% confidence level

2. $\alpha = 0.01$ (**1% Level**)

- More stringent criterion

- 1% chance of Type I error

- Used when more certainty is required

- Often used in medical research

- 99% confidence level

3. $\alpha = 0.001$ (**0.1% Level**)

- Highly stringent criterion

- 0.1% chance of Type I error

- Used for critical decisions

- Common in particle physics

- 99.9% confidence level

Thumb Rules for Significance Levels

Rules for significance levels encompass two key aspects: **selection guidelines** and **interpretation frameworks**. When selecting significance levels, researchers must make these decisions prior to conducting their study, ensuring alignment with established field standards and carefully considering the potential consequences of errors. The selection process should take into account both sample size and effect size, while remaining consistent with the overall research objectives. This proactive approach helps maintain scientific rigor and reduces the risk of post-hoc adjustments.

The interpretation framework provides clear decision rules for statistical significance. When the p-value is less than or equal to the chosen significance level (α), researchers ***reject the null hypothesis***, indicating ***statistical significance***.

Conversely, when the p-value exceeds α, researchers fail to reject the null hypothesis, suggesting a lack of statistical significance. It's crucial to understand that lowering the significance level (α) creates a trade-off: while it reduces Type I errors (false positives), it simultaneously increases the risk of Type II errors (false negatives).

Several important considerations guide the application of significance levels in research. Context plays a vital role, encompassing field-specific standards, research implications, the potential cost of errors, and sample size effects. Each field may have established conventions for significance levels based on historical precedent and practical requirements. Additionally, researchers must carefully weigh the implications of their findings and consider how sample size might influence their results.

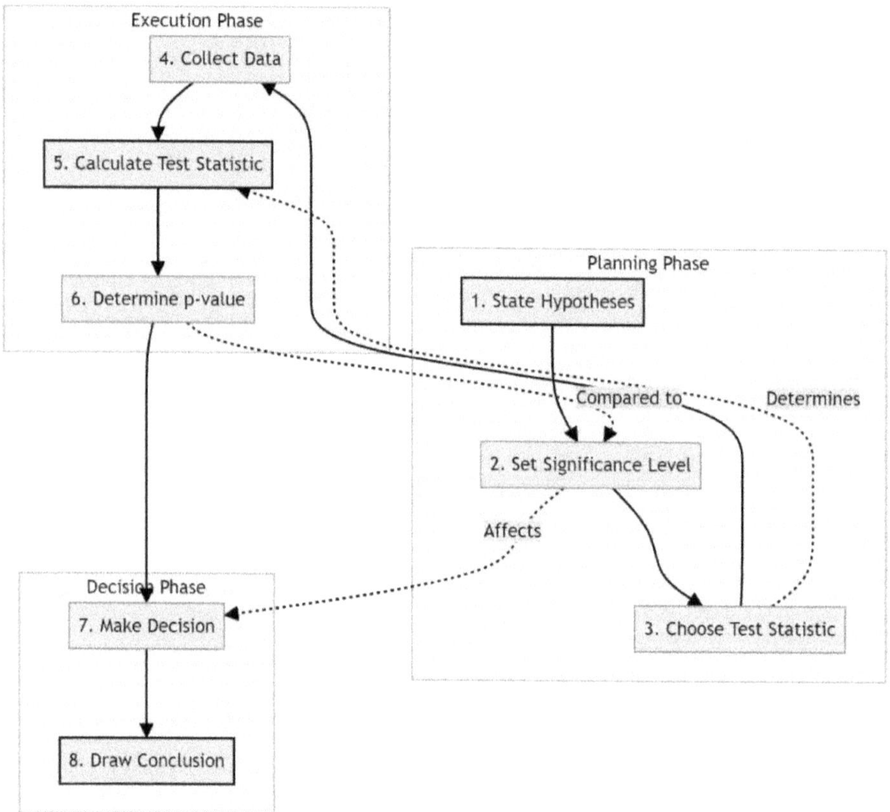

Fig. 6.2. Hypothesis Testing Process Flow

Understanding the limitations of significance testing is equally crucial. P-values and significance levels do not measure practical significance, and their interpretation can be heavily influenced by sample size. These statistical tools should never be used in isolation, as they fail to indicate effect size, which often provides more meaningful insights into the practical importance of research findings. This understanding helps researchers avoid common pitfalls in statistical interpretation.

Best practices in significance testing emphasize comprehensive reporting and thoughtful analysis. Researchers should always report exact p-values rather than simply stating whether results were significant. Multiple testing adjustments should be considered when appropriate, and effect sizes should be included to provide context for the findings. Discussion of practical significance helps bridge the gap between statistical significance and real-world implications. Acknowledging limitations and using appropriate significance levels for the specific research context ensures transparent and reliable research outcomes. This holistic approach to significance testing supports more robust and meaningful research conclusions.

The proper understanding and application of p-values and significance levels are essential for robust statistical analysis. While these tools provide valuable information for decision-making, they should be used as part of a comprehensive analytical approach that considers multiple factors and contextual elements.

6.3 Errors in Hypothesis Testing

Understanding potential errors in hypothesis testing is crucial for research design and interpretation.

In statistical hypothesis testing, researchers must navigate the complex landscape of potential errors while striving to make accurate and reliable conclusions. The fundamental understanding of **Type I** and **Type II errors**, along with **statistical power**, forms the cornerstone of robust research methodology and interpretation of results.

Type I errors, often denoted by α (*alpha*), occur when researchers *reject a true null hypothesis*, essentially discovering an effect that doesn't actually exist. This "*false positive*" represents one of the most concerning errors in research, as it can lead to incorrect conclusions and potentially harmful decisions. The probability of committing a Type I error is determined by the significance level, typically set at 0.05, meaning researchers accept a 5% chance of incorrectly rejecting a true null hypothesis. In fields where false positives could have serious consequences, such as medical research or safety testing, researchers often employ more stringent significance levels like 0.01 or 0.001.

Conversely, **Type II errors**, represented by β (*beta*), occur when researchers *fail to reject a false null hypothesis*, missing a genuine effect that actually exists. This "*false negative*" can be equally problematic, potentially leading to overlooked opportunities or failed detection of important relationships. *The probability of committing a Type II error is directly related to statistical power, which is defined as 1-β.* Understanding Type II errors is crucial because they often receive less attention than Type I errors, yet their consequences can be equally significant in research contexts.

Statistical power, a critical concept in hypothesis testing, represents the probability of correctly rejecting a false null hypothesis. In essence, it measures the likelihood of detecting an effect when it truly exists. Researchers typically aim for a power level of 0.80 (80%) or higher, indicating a strong ability to detect genuine effects. Power is influenced by several factors, including sample size, effect size, and the chosen significance level. Larger sample sizes generally increase power, as do larger effect sizes, while more stringent significance levels (smaller α) tend to reduce power.

The interrelationship between these concepts creates important trade-offs in research design. Decreasing the probability of Type I errors by using a more stringent significance level automatically increases the risk of Type II errors, potentially reducing the study's ability to detect genuine effects. This inverse relationship highlights the importance of careful consideration in research design, particularly in determining appropriate sample sizes and significance levels.

To effectively manage these potential errors, researchers employ various strategies. Power analysis conducted before the study helps determine appropriate sample sizes needed to detect effects of interest. Multiple testing adjustments can help control Type I error rates when conducting numerous statistical tests. Effect size calculations provide additional context for interpreting results beyond mere statistical significance.

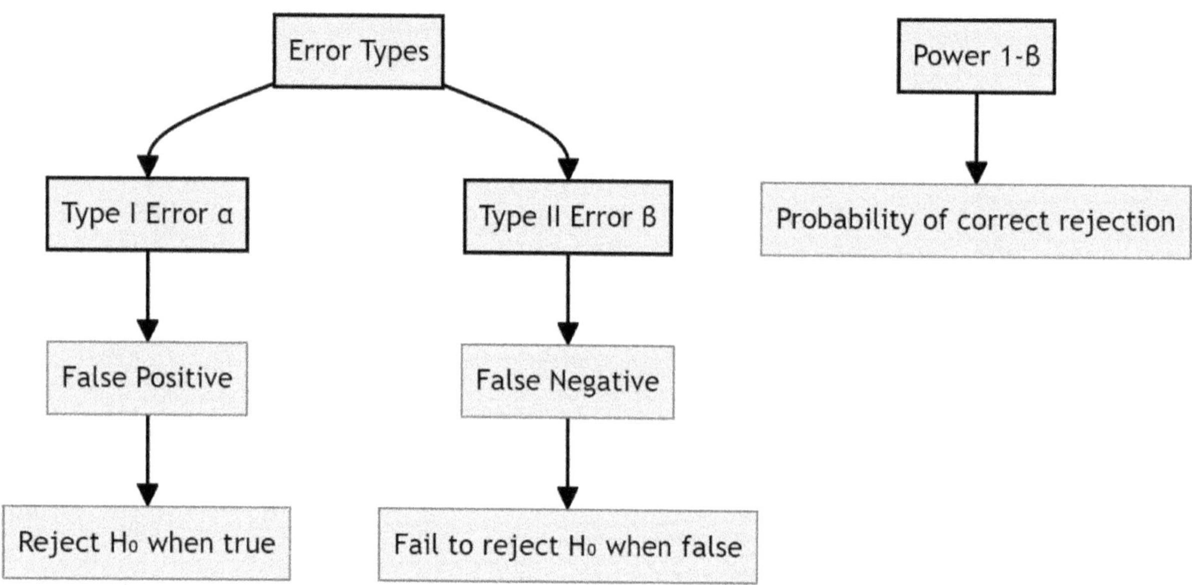

Fig. 6.3. Types of Errors in Hypothesis Testing

Best practices in hypothesis testing emphasize transparent reporting of both significant and non-significant results, along with comprehensive documentation of study parameters affecting error rates. Researchers should clearly state their chosen significance levels, provide power calculations, and discuss potential implications of both Type I and Type II errors in their specific research context. This approach ensures that readers can properly evaluate the strength of conclusions and make informed decisions based on the research findings.

The careful balance of Type I errors, Type II errors, and statistical power remains fundamental to quality research design and interpretation. Understanding these concepts helps researchers make informed decisions about study design and provides a framework for evaluating research findings critically and contextually.

6.4 Common Statistical Tests for Hypothesis Testing

The selection of appropriate statistical tests is crucial for valid hypothesis testing. Different tests serve different purposes and have specific assumptions that must be met.

Test Type	Purpose	Assumptions	Data Requirements	Example Application	Key Statistics
Parametric Tests					
Independent t-test	Compare means of two independent groups	• Normal distribution • Equal variances • Independent samples	Continuous data	Comparing drug vs. placebo	t-statistic, df, p-value
Paired t-test	Compare means of paired observations	• Normal distribution of differences • Paired measurements	Continuous data	Before/after treatment	t-statistic, df, p-value
One-way ANOVA	Compare means of 3+ groups	• Normal distribution • Equal variances • Independent samples	Continuous data	Comparing multiple treatments	F-statistic, df, p-value
Non-parametric Tests					
Mann-Whitney U	Compare distributions of two groups	• Independent samples • Ordinal or continuous data	Ranked data	Comparing symptom severity	U-statistic, p-value
Wilcoxon Signed-Rank	Compare paired observations	• Paired measurements • Ordinal or continuous data	Ranked data	Before/after symptom scores	W-statistic, p-value
Kruskal-Wallis	Compare distributions of 3+ groups	• Independent samples • Ordinal or continuous data	Ranked data	Comparing multiple treatments	H-statistic, p-value
Chi-square	Test association between categorical variables	• Independent observations • Expected frequencies >5	Categorical data	Disease association studies	χ^2, df, p-value

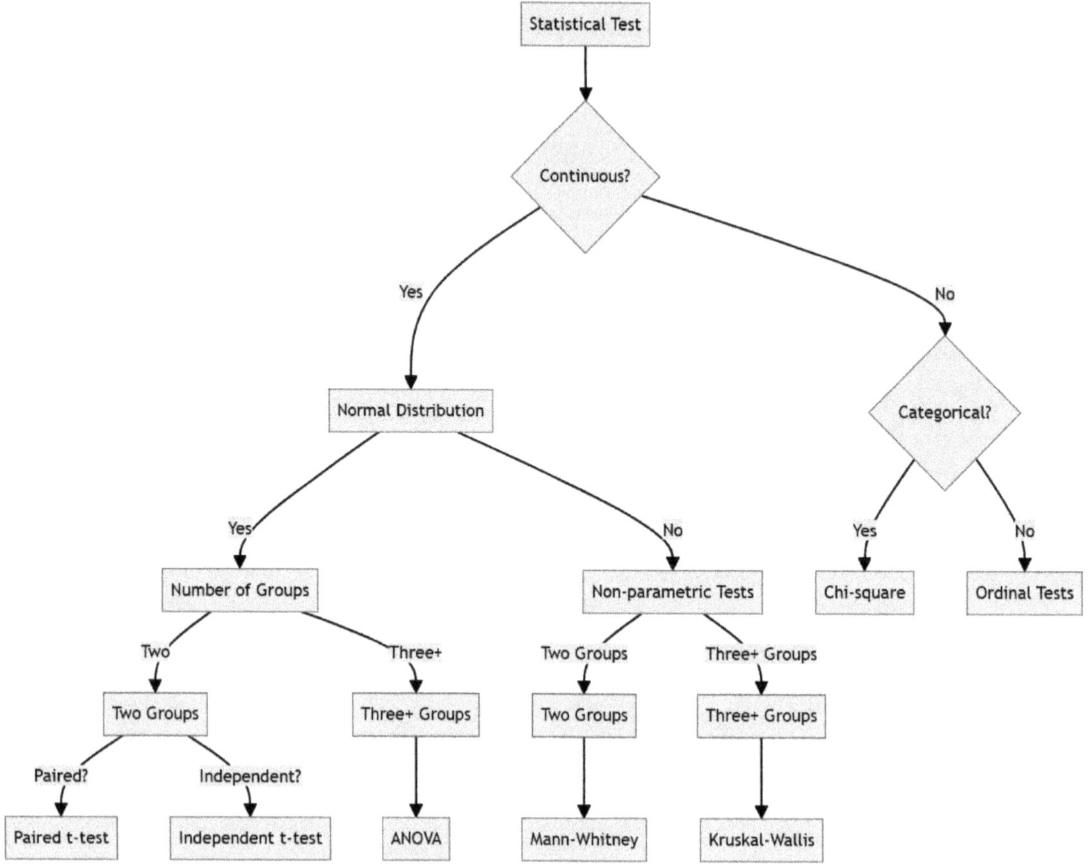

Fig. 6.4. Test Selection Decision Process

6.5 Interpretation of Hypothesis Test Results

The interpretation of hypothesis test results requires a nuanced understanding of both statistical and practical significance, establishing a comprehensive framework for meaningful research conclusions. This dual approach ensures that findings are not only statistically valid but also practically relevant in real-world applications.

Statistical significance, primarily assessed through p-values and confidence intervals, provides the foundation for initial interpretation. P-values, evaluated against predetermined thresholds (typically 0.05, 0.01, or 0.001), offer insights into the probability of obtaining observed results under the null hypothesis. However, these interpretations must consider multiple testing scenarios, where adjustments like Bonferroni correction help maintain appropriate error rates. *Sample size significantly influences p-values*, with larger samples potentially leading to statistically significant results even for minor effects. Confidence intervals complement p-values by providing a range of plausible values for the parameter of interest, offering both statistical significance information and practical insight into effect magnitude.

Practical significance extends beyond statistical measures to evaluate real-world impact through effect size measures and clinical relevance. Effect size metrics, such as Cohen's d for t-tests, η^2 for ANOVA, and odds ratios for categorical data, quantify the magnitude of observed differences or relationships. These standardized measures facilitate comparison across studies and provide context for interpreting results. In clinical settings, the concept of minimum clinically important difference (MCID) becomes crucial, helping determine whether statistically significant results translate to meaningful patient outcomes.

The integration of statistical and practical significance requires careful consideration of context-specific factors. Risk-benefit analysis and cost considerations play vital roles in determining the practical utility of findings. Researchers must balance statistical evidence with practical constraints, resource limitations, and potential implementation challenges. This comprehensive approach ensures that research conclusions not only meet rigorous statistical standards but also provide actionable insights for practitioners and stakeholders in the field.

Reporting Guidelines

Professional reporting of statistical results demands a structured and comprehensive approach that ensures clarity, reproducibility, and practical relevance. A well-crafted statistical report begins with a clear test description, including the specific test name, verification of assumptions, and software details, providing readers with essential context for understanding the analysis. The presentation of test statistics follows a standardized format, incorporating test values, degrees of freedom, and precise p-values, enabling readers to evaluate the statistical significance independently.

Results Reporting Template		
Element	**Required Information**	**Example**
Test Description	• Test name • Assumptions checked • Software used	"An independent-samples t-test was conducted using R (version 4.1.2)"
Test Statistics	• Test statistic • Degrees of freedom • P-value	"t(58) = 2.34, p = 0.023"
Effect Sizes	• Effect size measure • Confidence intervals	"Cohen's d = 0.61, 95% CI [0.08, 1.13]"
Descriptive Stats	• Group means/medians • Standard deviations • Sample sizes	"Treatment group (M = 12.5, SD = 3.8, n = 30)"
Visual Elements	• Appropriate graphs • Error bars • Clear labels	"Figure 1: Box plot showing distribution of responses"
Practical Impact	• Clinical significance • Real-world implications • Limitations	"The observed 25% improvement exceeds the minimal clinically important difference of 15%"

Effect sizes and their confidence intervals form a crucial component of modern statistical reporting, moving beyond mere significance testing to quantify the magnitude of observed effects. Comprehensive reporting includes detailed descriptive statistics for all groups, presenting means or medians, standard deviations, and sample sizes. Visual elements complement numerical results, with appropriate graphs, error bars, and clear labeling enhancing understanding of data patterns and relationships.

The translation of statistical findings into practical implications represents the culmination of effective reporting. This includes discussing clinical significance, real-world applications, and study limitations. By addressing both statistical and practical significance, researchers provide stakeholders with the necessary information to evaluate findings' relevance to their specific contexts. This comprehensive approach ensures that statistical reports serve their fundamental purpose: clear communication of research findings to inform evidence-based decision-making.

This comprehensive approach to hypothesis testing provides researchers with the tools needed to design, execute, and interpret their studies effectively. The integration of statistical rigor with practical significance ensures that research findings contribute meaningfully to scientific knowledge and practical applications.

7. Ethical Considerations in Research

Research is to discover facts that support a hypothesis, not to search for facts that prove it.

-   Fred Brooks

Ethics forms the cornerstone of responsible research in life sciences, ensuring that scientific advancement proceeds while respecting fundamental human and animal rights. This chapter explores the essential ethical principles and practices that guide modern research.

7.1 Importance of Ethics in Life Sciences Research

Ethics in life sciences research represents a cornerstone of responsible scientific investigation, built upon historical lessons and shaped by evolving understanding of moral obligations in scientific pursuits. The three fundamental principles - autonomy, beneficence, and justice - form an interconnected framework that guides ethical research practices.

7.1.1 Respect for Autonomy

The principle of autonomy holds paramount importance in research ethics, emphasizing the fundamental right of individuals to make informed decisions about their participation in research. This principle manifests through several key aspects of research conduct. Informed consent represents the practical application of autonomy, requiring clear communication of research purposes, procedures, risks, and benefits to potential participants. This process must ensure that participants understand their right to withdraw from research at any time without negative consequences.

Autonomy extends beyond initial consent to encompass ongoing respect for participant decisions throughout the research process. Researchers must maintain transparent communication, providing updates about any changes in research procedures or newly discovered risks. The protection of participant privacy and confidentiality also falls under this principle, requiring careful handling of personal information and research data.

7.1.2 Beneficence and Non-maleficence

The principle of beneficence requires researchers to maximize potential benefits while minimizing possible harms. This dual obligation encompasses both the positive duty to promote well-being and the negative duty to avoid harm. In practice, this requires careful risk-benefit analysis before initiating any research project. Researchers must critically evaluate whether potential benefits justify any risks to participants or society.

Non-maleficence, often considered alongside beneficence, specifically emphasizes the obligation to avoid harm. This principle requires researchers to implement appropriate safeguards, monitor for adverse effects, and maintain procedures for addressing unexpected negative outcomes. The application of this principle extends beyond individual participants to consider potential environmental impacts and broader societal implications of research.

7.1.3 Justice in Research

The principle of justice in research ethics focuses on fair distribution of both benefits and burdens of research. This encompasses several dimensions of fairness: in participant selection, in resource allocation, and in the distribution of research benefits. Researchers must ensure that vulnerable populations are not unduly burdened by research participation while being appropriately represented in research that might benefit them.

Justice also requires consideration of access to research benefits. This includes ensuring that populations who bear the burdens of research have the opportunity to benefit from research outcomes. The principle extends to considerations of global justice, particularly in international research collaborations where resource disparities might affect ethical conduct.

7.1.4 Historical Context and Evolution

The development of these ethical principles emerged from historical instances of research misconduct and abuse. The Nuremberg Code, established following World War II, represented a watershed moment in research ethics, establishing voluntary consent as an absolute requirement. The Declaration of Helsinki further developed these principles, providing specific guidelines for medical research involving human subjects.

The Belmont Report, published in 1979, formally articulated the three core principles and their applications to research practice. This document continues to influence current ethical frameworks while adapting to new challenges presented by advancing scientific capabilities.

7.1.5 Contemporary Challenges and Evolution

Modern advances in life sciences research present new ethical challenges requiring careful consideration and application of these fundamental principles. Genetic research, for example, raises questions about individual privacy and the right to know or not know genetic information. Biobanking and big data research challenge traditional concepts of informed consent and privacy protection.

Emerging technologies such as CRISPR gene editing and artificial intelligence in biological research present novel ethical considerations. These advances require careful application of traditional ethical principles while considering new dimensions of responsibility and potential impact.

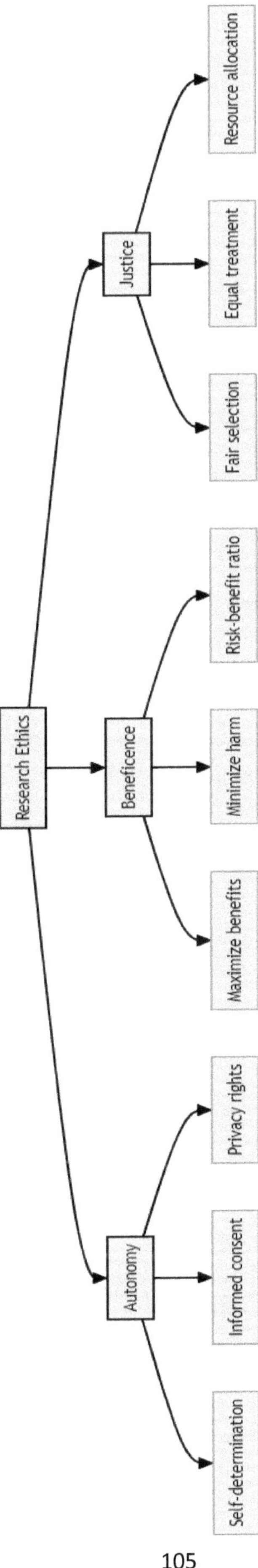

Fig. 7.1. Core Ethical Principles in Research

7.1.6 Implementation and Oversight

The practical implementation of ethical principles requires robust institutional frameworks and oversight mechanisms. Institutional Review Boards (IRBs) play a crucial role in ensuring ethical compliance, reviewing research proposals against established ethical guidelines. These bodies must balance protecting participant rights with enabling valuable scientific investigation.

Continuous education and training in research ethics helps maintain awareness and understanding of ethical obligations among researchers. This includes regular updates on evolving ethical considerations and new guidelines responding to advancing scientific capabilities.

7.1.7 Future Directions

The future of research ethics in life sciences must address emerging challenges while maintaining commitment to core principles. This includes developing new frameworks for ethical assessment of novel technologies and research approaches. International collaboration in establishing ethical guidelines becomes increasingly important as research becomes more globally interconnected.

Success in ethical research requires ongoing commitment to these fundamental principles while adapting to new challenges and opportunities. Through careful attention to ethical considerations and continuous evolution of ethical frameworks, researchers can ensure that scientific advancement proceeds with appropriate protection of individual rights and societal interests.

The importance of ethics in life sciences research extends beyond regulatory compliance to fundamental questions of human dignity and scientific responsibility. By maintaining strong ethical foundations while adapting to new challenges, researchers can ensure that scientific progress serves human welfare while respecting individual rights and dignity.

7.2 Ethical Considerations with Human Participants

The protection of human participants represents a fundamental obligation in research. This includes ensuring informed consent, maintaining confidentiality, and protecting privacy.

Historical Cases and Their Impact on Research Ethics				
Historical Case	**Time Period**	**Ethical Violations**	**Impact on Modern Ethics**	**Resulting Guidelines**
Nuremberg Medical Trials	1945-1946	• Forced experimentation • Inhumane treatment • Lack of consent	• Establishment of voluntary consent • Protection of human rights • Research justification requirements	Nuremberg Code (1947)
Tuskegee Syphilis Study	1932-1972	• Withholding treatment • Deception • Exploitation of vulnerable populations	• Informed consent requirements • Equal treatment principles • Protection of vulnerable groups	Belmont Report (1979)
Willowbrook Hepatitis Study	1955-1970	• Exploitation of disabled children • Questionable consent • Unnecessary exposure to harm	• Special protections for vulnerable populations • Stricter consent requirements • Risk-benefit assessment	Federal regulations for human subjects
HeLa Cells Case	1951	• Lack of consent • Privacy violations • Benefit sharing issues	• Tissue ownership rights • Privacy protections • Genetic information guidelines	HIPAA Privacy Rule Common Rule updates
Guatemala STD Studies	1946-1948	• Intentional infection • Lack of consent • International exploitation	• International research standards • Cross-border protection • Collaborative research guidelines	International ethical guidelines

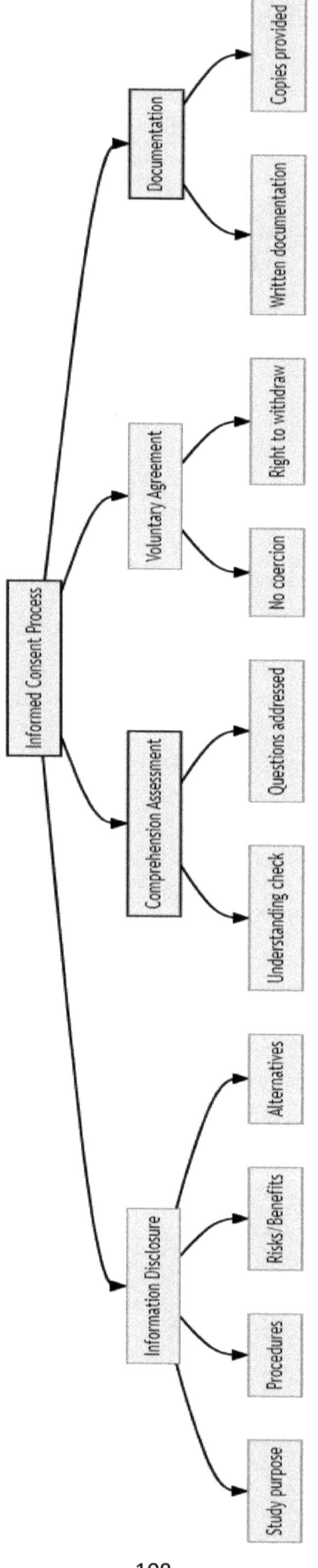

Fig. 7.2. Informed Consent Process

Special Considerations for Vulnerable Populations			
Children	**Pregnant Women**	**Prisoners**	**Cognitively Impaired**
• Parental consent requirements	• Fetal risk assessment	• Coercion prevention	• Capacity assessment
• Age-appropriate assent	• Benefit requirements	• Limited research scope	• Surrogate decision-makers
• Additional safeguards	• Partner involvement	• Justice requirements	• Enhanced protections

7.3 Ethical Considerations with Animal Subjects

Animal research ethics represents a critical domain in life sciences research, requiring careful balance between advancing scientific knowledge and ensuring humane treatment of animal subjects. The 3Rs framework - Replacement, Reduction, and Refinement - provides fundamental principles guiding ethical animal research practices.

7.3.1 Replacement: Seeking Alternatives to Animal Testing

The principle of Replacement emphasizes the obligation to use non-animal alternatives whenever scientifically valid. This principle operates at two levels: absolute replacement and relative replacement.

Absolute Replacement involves completely avoiding animal use through:

- Computer modeling and simulation
- In vitro studies using cell cultures
- Human volunteers for non-invasive studies
- Molecular and biochemical techniques
- Microorganisms or lower organisms

Relative Replacement includes:

- Using less sentient animals
- Employing early developmental stages
- Working with isolated organs or tissues
- Utilizing post-mortem material
- Implementing ex vivo approaches

7.3.2 Reduction: Minimizing Animal Numbers

The Reduction principle focuses on minimizing the number of animals used while maintaining scientific validity. This requires careful attention to experimental design and statistical considerations.

Statistical approaches to reduction include:

- Power analysis for sample size determination
- Factorial experimental designs
- Sequential sampling methods
- Advanced statistical techniques
- Pilot studies for parameter estimation

Experimental design strategies encompass:

- Sharing control groups
- Longitudinal studies versus cross-sectional
- Multiple outcome measures per animal
- Standardization of procedures
- Quality control measures

7.3.3 Refinement: Minimizing Pain and Distress

Refinement addresses the quality of animal life during research, focusing on minimizing pain, suffering, and distress while enhancing welfare.

Pain management strategies include:

- Appropriate anesthesia protocols
- Regular pain assessment
- Preventive analgesia
- Humane endpoints
- Post-procedure care

Environmental refinements encompass:

- Enhanced housing conditions

- Environmental enrichment

- Social housing when appropriate

- Temperature and humidity control

- Appropriate lighting cycles

7.3.4 Implementation and Oversight in Animal Research Ethics

The practical implementation of ethical principles in animal research demands a systematic, multi-phase approach that encompasses all stages of research activity. During the planning phase, researchers must conduct thorough literature reviews to identify potential alternatives to animal testing, actively consult with animal welfare experts, and optimize statistical design to ensure minimal animal usage while maintaining scientific validity. Protocol refinement at this stage requires careful consideration of all procedures, with particular attention to minimizing potential distress or discomfort. Resource assessment ensures that all necessary facilities, equipment, and expertise are available before research initiation.

The execution phase focuses on the actual implementation of research protocols with strict attention to animal welfare. This phase requires comprehensive staff training to ensure competency in all procedures, along with robust monitoring protocols to track animal well-being throughout the study. Welfare assessment must be ongoing and systematic, supported by detailed documentation systems that capture all relevant observations and interventions. Quality control measures during this phase help maintain consistency and adherence to approved protocols while allowing for rapid response to any concerns that arise.

The assessment phase provides crucial feedback for continuous improvement of animal research practices. This includes thorough evaluation of research outcomes, comprehensive analysis of welfare impacts, and further refinement of protocols based on practical experience. Reporting requirements must be met with complete and accurate documentation, and knowledge gained from the research experience should be shared to benefit future studies and improve animal welfare practices across the field.

Institutional oversight plays a fundamental role in ensuring ethical compliance and maintaining high standards in animal research. The Institutional Animal Care and Use Committee (IACUC) bears primary responsibility for protocol review and approval, ensuring compliance with all relevant regulations and ethical guidelines. Their oversight extends to monitoring ongoing research activities, overseeing staff training programs, conducting regular facility inspections, and developing institutional policies that promote animal welfare while supporting valid scientific research.

Facility requirements form another crucial component of institutional support for ethical animal research. This includes maintaining appropriate housing systems that meet or exceed species-specific requirements, implementing effective environmental controls to ensure animal comfort and well-being, providing comprehensive veterinary support, establishing clear emergency procedures, and maintaining detailed record-keeping systems that document all aspects of animal care and use.

Professional development and training represent ongoing commitments in ethical animal research. Staff members must maintain proficiency in animal handling techniques specific to each species involved in research, understand and apply appropriate pain assessment methods, and demonstrate competency in ethical decision-making. Training programs must also keep pace with new methodologies and best practices as they emerge in the field.

Documentation and reporting requirements provide essential accountability and transparency in animal research. These include maintaining detailed protocols for all procedures, conducting and recording regular welfare assessments, promptly reporting any adverse events, maintaining comprehensive monitoring records, and documenting research outcomes. This documentation serves both regulatory compliance and continuous improvement purposes.

Future directions in animal ethics continue to evolve with advancing technology and changing societal expectations. The integration of new technologies offers opportunities for improved welfare monitoring and reduced animal use. Validation of alternative methods remains a priority, along with efforts to harmonize standards internationally. Development of more sophisticated welfare assessment tools and increased emphasis on public transparency reflect growing awareness of the importance of ethical considerations in animal research.

Success in animal research ethics requires ongoing commitment to several key elements: continuous evaluation and improvement of research practices, regular updates to protocols based on new information and experience, active engagement of all staff members in maintaining high ethical standards, appropriate allocation of resources to support ethical practices, and effective communication with the public about the importance and conduct of animal research. Through this comprehensive approach, institutions can maintain high ethical standards while advancing scientific knowledge through animal research.

The implementation of the 3Rs framework represents an ongoing commitment to ethical animal research while advancing scientific knowledge. Through careful attention to these principles and continuous improvement efforts, researchers can maintain high ethical standards while conducting valuable scientific investigations.

This balanced approach ensures that animal research, when necessary, proceeds with maximum consideration for animal welfare while maintaining scientific validity and relevance.

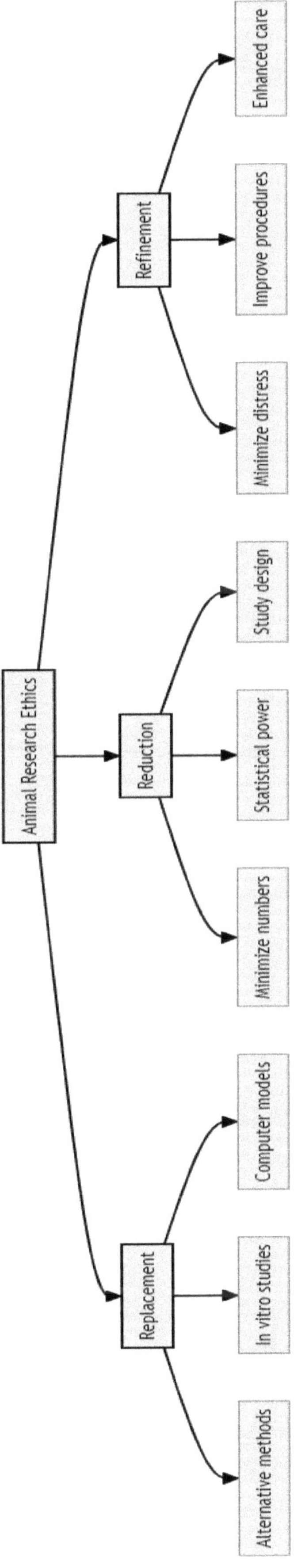

Fig. 7.3. The 3Rs of Animal Research Ethics

IACUC Responsibilities and Functions			
Function	**Description**	**Key Activities**	**Documentation Requirements**
Protocol Review	Evaluation of proposed animal research	• Scientific merit assessment • Ethics evaluation • Methodology review	• Detailed protocol • Justification forms • Amendment records
Facility Inspection	Regular monitoring of animal facilities	• Bi-annual inspections • Environmental monitoring • Health checks	• Inspection reports • Deficiency documentation • Correction plans
Policy Development	Creation and updating of institutional guidelines	• SOP development • Policy updates • Training requirements	• Policy manual • Training records • Compliance reports
Compliance Monitoring	Ensuring adherence to regulations and policies	• Protocol monitoring • Incident investigation • Reporting violations	• Monitoring logs • Investigation reports • Compliance records
Training Oversight	Management of training programs	• Required training • Continuing education • Competency assessment	• Training certificates • Competency records • Updates documentation

7.3.5 Committee for Control and Supervision of Experiments on Animals (CCSEA): Regulatory Framework and Guidelines

The Committee for Control and Supervision of Experiments on Animals (CCSEA) serves as the primary regulatory body overseeing animal experimentation in scientific research. Established under the Prevention of Cruelty to Animals Act 1960, CCSEA plays a crucial role in ensuring ethical treatment of animals in research while promoting scientific advancement through responsible experimentation.

The Prevention of Cruelty to Animals Act 1960 provides the legislative foundation for CCSEA's authority and operations. This landmark legislation establishes fundamental principles for animal welfare in research settings, emphasizing the need to prevent unnecessary suffering while recognizing the importance of scientific research. The Act mandates CCSEA's formation and empowers it to develop and enforce guidelines for animal experimentation, inspect facilities, and take action against violations of established standards.

CCSEA's regulatory framework encompasses several key aspects of animal experimentation. Registration requirements mandate that all institutions conducting animal research must obtain and maintain CCSEA registration. This process involves detailed evaluation of facility infrastructure, staff qualifications, and standard operating procedures. Regular renewal of registration ensures ongoing compliance with evolving standards and guidelines.

The breeding and sourcing of laboratory animals fall under strict CCSEA regulation. Guidelines specify requirements for breeding facilities, including environmental conditions, genetic maintenance, and health monitoring. Only CCSEA-registered facilities may breed animals for research purposes, ensuring quality control and traceable sourcing of research animals. These regulations help maintain standardization in research while protecting animal welfare.

Experimental procedures receive particular attention in CCSEA guidelines. The regulations detail permitted and prohibited procedures, requirements for anesthesia and analgesia, and criteria for humane endpoints. Specific attention is given to minimizing pain and distress through appropriate technique selection and refinement. The guidelines emphasize the importance of pilot studies and careful experimental design to minimize animal usage while maintaining scientific validity.

Personnel qualifications and training requirements form another crucial component of CCSEA regulations. All individuals involved in animal experimentation must demonstrate appropriate training and competency. This includes researchers, technical staff, and animal care personnel. Continuing education requirements ensure ongoing awareness of best practices and emerging welfare considerations.

Facility standards receive comprehensive coverage in CCSEA guidelines. Requirements address housing conditions, environmental controls, sanitation procedures, and veterinary care. Specific standards exist for different species, recognizing varying needs for space, social interaction, and environmental enrichment. Emergency preparedness and response procedures must be established and maintained.

Record-keeping requirements ensure transparency and accountability in animal research. Detailed documentation must be maintained for all aspects of animal care and use, including health records, experimental procedures, and outcome measures. These records facilitate both internal quality control and external inspection processes, providing evidence of compliance with established standards.

Transportation guidelines protect animal welfare during movement between facilities. Requirements address container specifications, environmental conditions during transport, and documentation requirements. Special attention is given to minimizing stress during transportation while ensuring animal safety and security.

Ethical review procedures form a cornerstone of CCSEA oversight. Institutional Animal Ethics Committees (IAECs) must be established in all research facilities, operating under CCSEA guidelines. These committees review research proposals, monitor ongoing studies, and ensure compliance with ethical standards. CCSEA provides detailed guidelines for IAEC composition, functioning, and responsibilities.

The application of the 3Rs principle (Replacement, Reduction, Refinement) receives strong emphasis in CCSEA guidelines. Researchers must demonstrate consideration of alternatives to animal use, justify proposed animal numbers through statistical analysis, and implement refined procedures to minimize suffering. Regular review of these aspects ensures ongoing commitment to animal welfare principles.

Inspection and monitoring procedures enable CCSEA oversight of research facilities. Regular inspections assess compliance with established standards, while surprise visits help ensure consistent adherence to requirements. Non-compliance may result in corrective actions, suspension of research activities, or revocation of facility registration.

Recent updates to CCSEA guidelines reflect evolving understanding of animal welfare needs and advancing research capabilities. These include enhanced requirements for environmental enrichment, expanded pain management protocols, and updated criteria for humane endpoints. Regular guideline revision ensures incorporation of new scientific knowledge and changing ethical considerations.

International harmonization efforts influence CCSEA guidelines, promoting alignment with global standards while maintaining appropriate local context. Collaboration with international organizations facilitates knowledge exchange and standard development. This approach helps ensure that Indian research maintains international acceptability while meeting national requirements.

Enforcement mechanisms include both routine monitoring and complaint investigation procedures. CCSEA has authority to take action against violations, ranging from corrective action requirements to legal proceedings under the Prevention of Cruelty to Animals Act. This enforcement authority ensures guideline compliance while protecting animal welfare.

Public transparency requirements promote accountability in animal research. Institutions must maintain publicly accessible information about their animal use and care programs. This transparency helps maintain public trust while promoting understanding of the role of animal research in scientific advancement.

Success in implementing CCSEA guidelines requires ongoing commitment from research institutions and personnel. Regular training, robust quality control programs, and effective communication systems help ensure consistent compliance with established standards. Through careful attention to these requirements, institutions can maintain high ethical standards while conducting valuable scientific research using animal subjects.

7.4 Research Misconduct and Avoiding Bias

Research misconduct represents one of the most serious challenges to scientific integrity, potentially undermining public trust and compromising the advancement of knowledge. Understanding the nature of research misconduct, its various forms, and strategies for prevention is essential for maintaining the credibility and quality of scientific research.

7.4.1 Defining Research Misconduct

Research misconduct encompasses three primary categories of violations: fabrication, falsification, and plagiarism (FFP). Fabrication involves creating data or results and recording or reporting them as genuine research findings. This represents perhaps the most egregious form of misconduct, as it introduces completely fictional elements into the scientific record. Falsification includes manipulating research materials, equipment, or processes, as well as changing or omitting data in ways that misrepresent research findings. This form of misconduct may be more subtle than fabrication but is equally damaging to scientific integrity. Plagiarism, the appropriation of another person's ideas, processes, results, or words without giving appropriate credit, violates both ethical principles and intellectual property rights.

7.4.2 Contributing Factors to Research Misconduct

Several factors can contribute to research misconduct, including publication pressure, competition for funding, career advancement requirements, and institutional culture. The "publish or perish" environment in academia can create pressure to produce positive results quickly, potentially leading to corner-cutting or outright misconduct. Limited research funding and intense competition may tempt researchers to enhance or manipulate results to increase chances of funding success. Career advancement metrics that heavily emphasize publication quantity over quality might inadvertently incentivize misconduct.

7.4.3 Types of Bias in Research

Bias in research can manifest in various forms, some subtle and others more obvious. Selection bias occurs when study participants or data points are not representative of the intended population. Confirmation bias leads researchers to seek evidence supporting their hypotheses while overlooking contradictory data. Publication bias results in the preferential publication of positive results over negative findings, potentially skewing the scientific record. Measurement bias arises from systematic errors in data collection or analysis methods.

Common Types of Researcher Bias and Mitigation Strategies				
Bias Type	**Description**	**Examples**	**Prevention Strategies**	**Impact on Research**
Selection Bias	Systematic differences in sample selection	• Convenience sampling • Volunteer bias • Exclusion bias	• Random selection • Clear criteria • Representative sampling	Data generalizability
Confirmation Bias	Tendency to confirm preexisting beliefs	• Selective data use • Ignoring contradictions • Biased interpretation	• Pre-registered protocols • Blind analysis • External review	Result interpretation
Measurement Bias	Systematic errors in data collection	• Instrument bias • Observer bias • Response bias	• Standardized methods • Multiple observers • Calibration	Data accuracy
Reporting Bias	Selective reporting of outcomes	• Publication bias • Outcome reporting bias • Time lag bias	• Pre-registration • Complete reporting • Negative result inclusion	Literature reliability
Cultural Bias	Impact of cultural assumptions	• Language bias • Cultural assumptions • Ethnocentrism	• Cultural awareness • Diverse teams • Local consultation	Study validity

7.4.4 Prevention Strategies

Preventing research misconduct requires a multi-faceted approach involving individual researchers, institutions, and the broader scientific community. At the individual level, researchers must maintain rigorous documentation of all research activities, including raw data, analysis procedures, and decision-making processes. Laboratory notebooks, electronic records, and detailed protocols provide accountability and transparency.

Institutional measures should include comprehensive training programs in research ethics and integrity. These programs must go beyond simple rule compliance to foster a deep understanding of ethical principles and their practical application. Clear policies and procedures for reporting suspected misconduct, protecting whistleblowers, and investigating allegations help create an environment where integrity is valued and protected.

7.4.5 Quality Control Measures

Implementation of robust quality control measures helps prevent both intentional misconduct and unintentional errors. These measures include peer review of protocols before study initiation, regular data audits, and validation of critical findings by independent team members. Statistical review of research designs and analysis plans can help identify potential sources of bias before they affect results.

7.4.6 Managing Detected Misconduct

When misconduct is detected, institutions must respond promptly and appropriately. This includes thorough investigation of allegations, protection of both whistleblowers and accused parties during investigations, and appropriate sanctions when misconduct is confirmed. The response must balance the need for justice with opportunities for rehabilitation and education.

A. Role of Mentorship

Effective mentorship plays a crucial role in preventing research misconduct and bias. Senior researchers must model ethical behavior and create an environment where questions about ethical issues are welcomed and addressed openly. Regular discussions about research integrity, proper data management, and ethical decision-making should be integrated into research training.

B. Institutional Culture

Creating and maintaining a culture of integrity requires consistent commitment from institutional leadership. This includes providing adequate resources for proper research conduct, recognizing and rewarding ethical behavior, and ensuring that productivity pressures do not compromise integrity. Open communication channels and regular forums for discussing ethical issues help maintain awareness and engagement.

C. Documentation and Transparency

Maintaining detailed documentation of research activities supports both integrity and reproducibility. This includes preserving raw data, documenting all analytical steps, and maintaining clear records of decision-making processes. Transparency in reporting negative or unexpected results helps prevent bias in the scientific record.

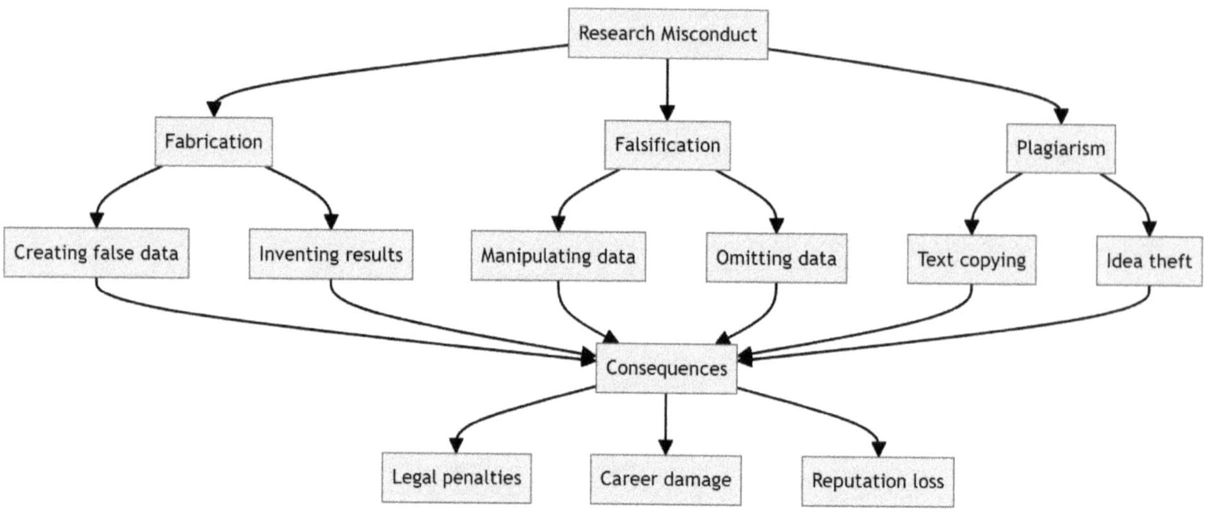

Fig. 7.4. Types and Implications of Research Misconduct

7.4.7 Future Directions

Advancing technology creates both new opportunities for misconduct and new tools for prevention and detection. Digital tools for data management and analysis can include built-in quality controls and audit trails. However, these same technologies may create new forms of potential misconduct that require vigilance and updated prevention strategies.

Success in preventing research misconduct and bias requires ongoing commitment to integrity at all levels of the scientific enterprise. Through comprehensive training, robust institutional support, and consistent application of prevention strategies, the research community can maintain high standards of scientific integrity while advancing knowledge through ethical investigation.

7.5 Navigating Ethical Approvals and Review Boards

The ethical review process represents a critical checkpoint in research, ensuring protection of human subjects while maintaining scientific integrity and regulatory compliance. This systematic review process, typically conducted through Institutional Review Boards (IRBs), serves as a guardian of research ethics and participant safety.

The IRB review process follows a structured pathway designed to thoroughly evaluate research proposals while maintaining efficiency. Initial submission requires careful preparation of comprehensive documentation that demonstrates both scientific merit and ethical considerations. Upon receipt, the IRB conducts preliminary screening to ensure completeness of submission materials and appropriateness for review. This initial assessment determines whether the proposal qualifies for expedited review or requires full board evaluation.

Essential Documentation for Ethical Review			
Document Type	**Purpose**	**Key Components**	**Review Considerations**
Research Protocol	Detailed study plan	• Background • Methodology • Risk management • Data handling	• Scientific merit • Risk-benefit ratio • Feasibility
Informed Consent	Participant agreement	• Study information • Rights explanation • Contact details • Signature forms	• Readability • Completeness • Language options
Safety Monitoring	Risk management	• Adverse event reporting • Safety procedures • Emergency protocols	• Adequacy • Implementation • Response time
Data Protection	Privacy safeguards	• Storage methods • Access controls • Confidentiality measures	• Security level • HIPAA compliance • Data lifecycle
Training Records	Personnel qualifications	• Ethics training • Protocol training • Safety training	• Currency • Completeness • Relevance
Progress Reports	Study monitoring	• Enrollment updates • Safety reports • Protocol deviations	• Timeliness • Completeness • Problem resolution

Essential documentation forms the foundation of ethical review, with each component serving specific purposes in demonstrating research integrity and participant protection. The research protocol stands as the cornerstone document, providing detailed information about study background, methodology, and implementation plans. This comprehensive document must clearly articulate the scientific rationale while demonstrating thoughtful consideration of potential risks and their management. Review committees evaluate protocols for scientific merit, feasibility, and appropriate risk-benefit balance.

Informed consent documentation represents another crucial element in the ethical review process. These documents must clearly communicate study information, participant rights, and contact details in language accessible to potential participants. Review committees carefully assess consent documents for readability, completeness, and availability in appropriate languages for the target population. The consent process must demonstrate respect for participant autonomy while ensuring comprehensive understanding of study participation implications.

Safety monitoring plans detail procedures for protecting participant wellbeing throughout the study. These documents outline adverse event reporting procedures, safety monitoring protocols, and emergency response plans. Review committees evaluate these plans for adequacy, implementation feasibility, and appropriate response timing. Regular safety updates during study implementation ensure ongoing protection of participant interests.

Data protection measures receive particular scrutiny during ethical review. Documentation must detail methods for securing participant information, controlling access to research data, and maintaining confidentiality throughout the study lifecycle. Review committees assess these measures against current security standards and regulatory requirements, including HIPAA compliance where applicable. The evaluation considers both technical and procedural aspects of data protection.

Training records demonstrate research team qualifications and preparedness for study implementation. Documentation must verify completion of required ethics training, protocol-specific instruction, and safety procedures. Review committees assess the currency and relevance of training while ensuring comprehensive coverage of essential topics. Ongoing training requirements ensure maintained competency throughout study duration.

Progress reporting requirements provide mechanisms for ongoing oversight of approved research. These reports include updates on enrollment progress, safety events, and protocol deviations. Review committees evaluate these reports for timeliness, completeness, and appropriate problem resolution. Regular monitoring ensures maintenance of ethical standards throughout study implementation.

The review process itself operates through careful evaluation of submission materials against established criteria. Committees consider scientific validity, risk-benefit ratio, participant protection measures, and regulatory compliance. This evaluation may involve multiple rounds of review and revision before final approval. The process ensures thorough consideration of all aspects while maintaining reasonable timelines for research progression.

Success in navigating ethical review requires careful attention to documentation requirements and review processes. Researchers must maintain open communication with review boards, responding promptly to questions or concerns. Regular updates during study implementation ensure ongoing compliance with approved protocols while allowing appropriate modification when needed.

Institutional support plays a crucial role in successful ethical review navigation. Resources for protocol development, documentation preparation, and ongoing compliance monitoring help ensure successful review outcomes. Training programs and consultation services support researchers in meeting ethical review requirements while maintaining research integrity.

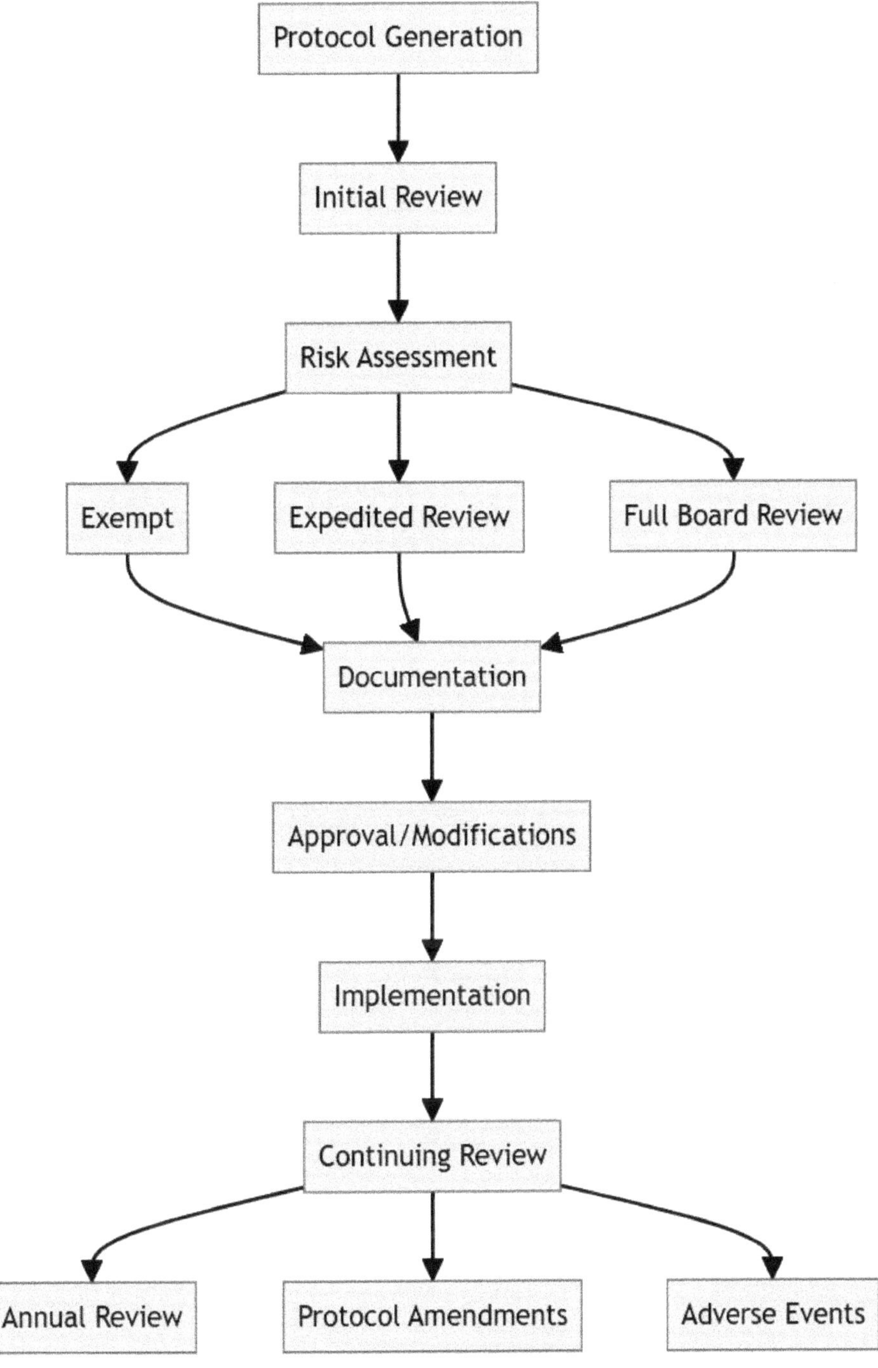

Fig. 7.5. IRB Review Process Flow

Through careful attention to documentation requirements and review processes, researchers can successfully navigate ethical approval while ensuring protection of research participants and maintenance of scientific integrity. This systematic approach helps advance scientific knowledge while upholding ethical principles in research conduct.

7.5.1 Ethical Review Categories and Considerations in Research

Understanding and navigating different categories of ethical review represents a crucial skill for researchers planning and implementing human subjects research. Each review category serves specific purposes, reflecting varying levels of risk and complexity in research protocols.

A. Exempt Review: Minimal Risk Studies

Exempt review applies to research activities presenting minimal risk to participants and falling within specific regulatory categories. Educational research, including studies of regular instructional strategies and effectiveness, typically qualifies for exempt review. This category also encompasses research involving observation of public behavior where participants remain anonymous and face no risk of harm. Analysis of existing data, particularly when publicly available or recorded without identifiers, often qualifies for exempt status.

Despite the term "exempt," these studies still require institutional review to confirm their qualification for this category. Researchers must submit sufficient documentation to demonstrate alignment with exempt criteria while maintaining ethical research practices. The exempt determination process typically proceeds more quickly than other review types, facilitating timely research initiation.

B. Expedited Review: Streamlined Process for Minimal Risk Research

Expedited review applies to research involving minimal risk procedures while requiring greater oversight than exempt studies. This category allows review by individual IRB members rather than requiring full board consideration. Common examples include blood sampling within specified limits, noninvasive physiological measurements, and data collection through moderate exercise by healthy volunteers.

Minor modifications to previously approved research often qualify for expedited review, streamlining the amendment process. Annual continuing reviews of minimal risk studies typically proceed through expedited mechanisms, maintaining appropriate oversight while reducing administrative burden. This category balances protection of participant interests with efficient review processes.

C. Full Board Review: Complex and Higher Risk Research

Full board review provides comprehensive evaluation of research involving greater than minimal risk or sensitive aspects requiring careful consideration. Studies involving vulnerable populations, such as children, prisoners, or individuals with impaired decision-making capacity, typically require full board review. Novel interventions or experimental procedures often necessitate this level of scrutiny to ensure adequate risk assessment and management.

Sensitive research topics, including studies of illegal activities, sexual behavior, or psychological stress, generally require full board review. This comprehensive evaluation ensures appropriate protection measures while considering broader ethical implications of proposed research.

7.5.2 Key Considerations for Successful Review

Successful navigation of ethical review processes requires careful attention to multiple factors affecting review outcomes and timing. Timeline management represents a crucial consideration, requiring awareness of submission deadlines, review cycle timing, and processing requirements for different submission types.

Communication strategy plays a vital role in successful review outcomes. Clear, well-organized documentation facilitates efficient review while demonstrating research team competence. Prompt responses to reviewer questions or concerns maintain review momentum while showing commitment to ethical research conduct. Regular updates during implementation demonstrate ongoing attention to participant protection and protocol compliance.

Quality control measures support successful ethical review and implementation. Protocol compliance requires systematic monitoring and documentation of research activities. Data integrity measures ensure reliable research outcomes while protecting participant interests. Safety monitoring procedures demonstrate commitment to participant protection throughout study implementation.

Risk management strategies address potential challenges during research implementation. Adverse event handling procedures ensure appropriate response to unexpected occurrences while maintaining participant safety. Protocol deviation management demonstrates ability to identify and address implementation challenges while maintaining research integrity. Systems for handling participant complaints ensure responsive attention to concerns while protecting participant rights.

7.5.3 Practical Implementation Strategies

Success in ethical review requires systematic attention to preparation and implementation details:

Documentation preparation must be thorough and organized, anticipating reviewer questions and concerns. This includes clear articulation of scientific rationale, risk management strategies, and participant protection measures.

Timeline planning should account for possible review cycles and revision requirements. Researchers should build adequate time into project schedules for thorough review processes, including potential requests for modification or clarification.

Communication systems must support efficient interaction with review boards and research teams. Regular team meetings ensure consistent protocol implementation while maintaining awareness of ethical requirements and safety measures.

Quality control measures require systematic implementation and documentation. Regular audits of research activities help ensure maintained compliance with approved protocols while identifying potential areas for improvement.

Through careful attention to these various aspects of ethical review, researchers can successfully navigate approval processes while ensuring protection of research participants and maintenance of scientific integrity. This systematic approach supports advancement of scientific knowledge while upholding ethical principles in research conduct.

8. Writing and Communicating Research Findings

The outcome of any serious research can only be to make two questions grow where only one grew before.

-   Thorstein Veblen

Scientific research achieves its full value only when effectively communicated to the broader scientific community. This chapter explores the essential elements of scientific writing and presentation in life sciences.

8.1 Introduction to Scientific Writing for Life Sciences

Scientific writing in the life sciences demands a specialized approach that combines technical accuracy with clear communication. This unique form of writing serves as the foundation for sharing complex biological research and advancing scientific knowledge through effective scholarly communication.

8.1.1 Fundamental Principles of Scientific Writing

The cornerstone of scientific writing lies in its precision. Every word must be carefully chosen to convey exact meaning, avoiding ambiguity and misinterpretation. Technical terms must be used accurately and consistently throughout the document, with clear definitions provided where necessary. This precision extends to numerical data presentation, requiring careful attention to significant figures, units, and statistical reporting conventions.

Clarity in scientific writing emerges from logical organization and straightforward expression of ideas. Complex biological concepts must be presented in a manner that guides readers through intricate details while maintaining clear connections between ideas. Writers must strike a delicate balance between providing sufficient detail for comprehension and avoiding overwhelming complexity that might obscure key messages.

Objectivity represents another fundamental principle of scientific writing. Researchers must present their findings without bias, acknowledging both supporting and contradicting evidence. This objective stance requires careful word choice to avoid implying certainty where uncertainty exists. Phrases like "the data suggest" or "the evidence indicates" often replace more definitive statements, reflecting the tentative nature of scientific conclusions.

8.1.2 Writing Conventions in Life Sciences

Voice and tense usage follow specific conventions in scientific writing. Methods sections typically employ passive voice to emphasize procedures rather than performers ("Samples were analyzed" rather than "We analyzed samples"). Results sections often use past tense to describe specific findings, while discussion sections may shift to present tense when discussing broader implications. These conventions help readers navigate different aspects of the research narrative.

Technical terminology requires consistent and precise application. Scientific names follow specific formatting rules (e.g., italicization of genus and species names). Abbreviations must be defined at first use and employed consistently thereafter. Gene and protein nomenclature must adhere to field-specific conventions, ensuring clarity and standardization across the scientific literature.

Data presentation follows strict conventions in life sciences writing. Numerical results require appropriate precision and consistent formatting. Statistical results must include specific elements such as test types, p-values, and effect sizes. Tables and figures demand clear labeling, with legends providing sufficient detail for standalone comprehension while maintaining concise presentation.

Sentence structure in scientific writing emphasizes clarity and efficiency. Complex ideas are often broken into manageable segments, with each sentence conveying a single main point. Parallel structure helps maintain clarity when presenting multiple related ideas or procedures. Transitional phrases guide readers through logical progressions of ideas while maintaining coherent flow.

Citation practices in life sciences writing follow field-specific conventions. In-text citations must accurately reflect source material while maintaining readable prose. Citation density often increases in introduction and discussion sections, demonstrating thorough engagement with existing literature while avoiding excessive disruption of narrative flow.

Paragraph organization follows logical progression of ideas. Each paragraph typically opens with a clear topic sentence, followed by supporting evidence and explanation. Concluding sentences often link to subsequent paragraphs, maintaining coherent flow throughout the document. This structured approach helps readers follow complex scientific arguments and relationships between ideas.

Visual element integration requires careful attention to placement and reference within the text. Figures and tables must be introduced before they appear, with clear explanation of their significance to the research narrative. References to visual elements should guide readers' attention to specific features while maintaining narrative flow.

Language precision extends beyond technical terminology to general writing clarity. Unnecessary words are eliminated, and complex phrases are simplified where possible. This concise approach helps maintain focus on essential information while reducing potential confusion or misinterpretation.

Verb choice in scientific writing emphasizes specific actions and relationships. Strong, precise verbs help convey research actions and findings clearly. Avoiding vague or weak verbs enhances writing impact while maintaining scientific accuracy.

Scientific Writing Conventions and Applications			
Convention	**Description**	**Examples**	**Common Errors to Avoid**
Voice	• Use of passive voice for methods • Active voice for conclusions • Consistent tense usage	• "Samples were analyzed..." • "The results show..." • "We conclude that..."	• Mixed tenses • Inconsistent voice • Personal pronouns in methods
Terminology	• Standard scientific terms • Defined abbreviations • Consistent nomenclature	• Scientific names in italics • Gene symbols in standard format • SI units	• Undefined abbreviations • Inconsistent formatting • Colloquial terms
Data Presentation	• Precise numerical reporting • Statistical significance • Appropriate figures/tables	• "$p < 0.05$" • Mean ± SD • 95% CI	• Imprecise measurements • Missing units • Inadequate statistics
Citation Style	• Journal-specific format • In-text citations • Reference list	• Harvard style • Vancouver system • APA format	• Inconsistent formatting • Missing references • Incorrect citations

Formatting conventions in life sciences writing extend to document structure and presentation. Consistent heading levels, spacing, and font usage help readers navigate complex documents efficiently. These formatting elements contribute to overall document accessibility while meeting professional publication standards.

Success in scientific writing requires careful attention to these principles and conventions while maintaining engaging presentation of complex ideas. Writers must continually balance technical accuracy with readability, ensuring effective communication of scientific findings to their intended audience. Through mastery of these elements, researchers can effectively contribute to the advancement of scientific knowledge in their field.

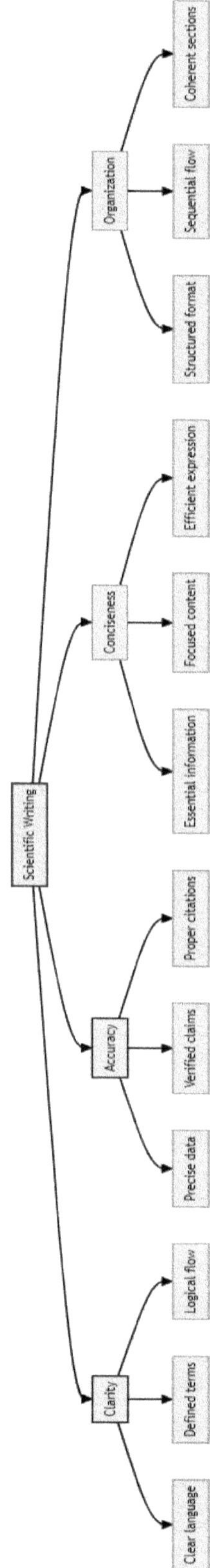

Fig. 8.1. Principles of Scientific Writing

The development of effective scientific writing skills requires practice and attention to evolving conventions within the field. Regular review of current literature helps writers stay current with accepted practices while developing their own clear and effective writing style. This ongoing process of refinement ensures that scientific writing continues to serve its essential role in advancing biological knowledge and understanding.

8.2 Structuring a Research Report

The organization of scientific research into a coherent, well-structured report represents a critical skill in academic and professional research. The IMRAD format provides a standardized framework that facilitates clear communication of research findings while ensuring comprehensive coverage of essential elements.

The **title** and **abstract** serve as the gateway to research reports, demanding particular attention despite their brevity. The title must precisely reflect the study's content while remaining concise and engaging. It should contain key terms that facilitate database searches and clearly indicate the research focus. The abstract provides a comprehensive yet concise summary of the entire study, typically structured to include background, objectives, methods, results, and conclusions within a strict word limit. This component often determines whether readers will proceed to the full article, making it crucial for clear, accurate, and engaging presentation of the research essence.

Introduction sections establish the foundation for understanding the research's significance and context. This section begins with a broad overview of the research area, gradually narrowing focus to specific research questions or hypotheses. The introduction must clearly articulate the research problem's significance, demonstrating its relevance to the field and potential contributions to existing knowledge. Literature review within the introduction should be selective and focused, providing essential background while avoiding exhaustive coverage. The section concludes with clear statements of research objectives and hypotheses, establishing precise expectations for the study's outcomes.

Methods sections require detailed yet efficient presentation of research procedures. This section must provide sufficient detail for replication while maintaining reader engagement. Researchers should clearly describe study design, participant selection criteria, data collection procedures, and analytical approaches. The description of methodological choices should include rationales, particularly for novel or complex procedures. Statistical analyses must be described with sufficient detail to allow verification of results, including software packages used and specific statistical tests employed. Ethical considerations and approval details should also be included where relevant.

Results sections focus on presenting findings clearly and objectively, without interpretation. This section requires careful organization of data, typically progressing from descriptive statistics to more complex analyses. Visual presentations through tables and figures should complement textual descriptions, with each element serving a specific purpose rather than duplicating information. Statistical results should be reported following field-specific conventions, including appropriate effect sizes and confidence intervals. Unexpected or negative results warrant equal attention to positive findings, maintaining scientific integrity through comprehensive reporting.

Discussion sections transform raw results into meaningful conclusions through careful interpretation and contextualization. This section begins by summarizing key findings without repeating detailed results. Interpretation should place findings within the context of existing literature, identifying areas of agreement and contradiction while explaining potential reasons for discrepancies. Theoretical implications should be explored thoroughly, considering how findings contribute to or challenge existing theoretical frameworks. Practical applications of research findings warrant careful consideration, including potential implementation challenges and recommendations.

The limitations section requires honest assessment of study constraints while maintaining confidence in research validity. Methodological limitations should be acknowledged transparently, including potential impacts on result interpretation. Sample limitations, such as size or composition, warrant careful discussion regarding generalizability. This section should also suggest how future research might address identified limitations, transforming constraints into opportunities for advancement.

Conclusions must concisely summarize the study's main contributions while avoiding overstatement. This section should clearly articulate the research's significance to the field, including both theoretical and practical implications. Future research directions should emerge logically from study findings and limitations, providing clear guidance for subsequent investigations.

References must follow precise formatting requirements while ensuring comprehensive coverage of relevant literature. Citation accuracy is crucial, with each reference contributing meaningfully to the research narrative. The reference list should demonstrate thorough engagement with current literature while acknowledging seminal works in the field.

Appendices provide space for detailed information that would disrupt main text flow. This might include detailed methodological protocols, raw data tables, or supplementary analyses. Each appendix should be clearly labeled and referenced within the main text, ensuring accessible organization of supplementary materials.

The effective structure of research reports requires careful attention to both content and presentation. Each section must fulfill its specific function while maintaining coherent flow throughout the document. Clear organization, precise language, and logical progression of ideas ensure that research findings are communicated effectively to the intended audience.

Success in research report structuring requires balance between comprehensiveness and clarity. Authors must provide sufficient detail for understanding and replication while maintaining reader engagement. Through careful attention to structural elements and content organization, researchers can effectively communicate their findings while contributing to scientific knowledge advancement in their field.

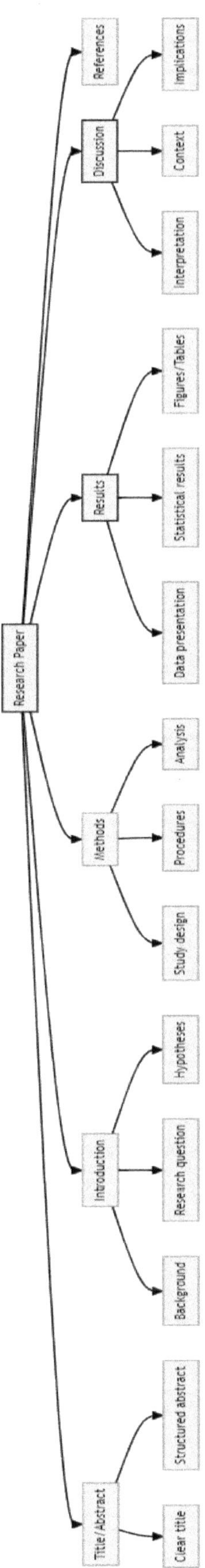

Fig. 8.2. Research Paper Structure

Formatting considerations, including headings, spacing, and visual element placement, contribute significantly to report accessibility. Consistent formatting throughout the document enhances readability while demonstrating professional attention to detail. Authors should carefully follow journal-specific guidelines while ensuring that formatting choices support clear communication of research content.

8.3 Guidelines for Literature Review

Literature reviews represent a foundational element of scientific research, providing comprehensive analysis and synthesis of existing knowledge in a field. A well-executed literature review requires systematic approaches, critical analysis skills, and effective organization of information to contribute meaningfully to scientific understanding.

The systematic approach to literature review begins with developing a clear and reproducible search strategy. This strategy must identify relevant databases, specific search terms, and appropriate combinations of keywords that capture the full scope of the research topic. Researchers should document their search methodology, including boolean operators used, filters applied, and any database-specific adaptations. This documentation ensures transparency and reproducibility while demonstrating the comprehensive nature of the review.

Inclusion and exclusion criteria form critical components of the systematic approach. These criteria must be established before beginning the review and should clearly specify which studies will be considered relevant. Typical criteria might include publication dates, research methodologies, sample characteristics, language of publication, and specific outcome measures. The rationale for each criterion should be clearly articulated and aligned with the review's objectives. This systematic filtering process helps maintain focus while ensuring comprehensive coverage of relevant literature.

Quality assessment of identified literature requires careful consideration of methodological rigor, sample size adequacy, and potential sources of bias. Researchers should employ standardized quality assessment tools appropriate to their field and research design. This assessment might include evaluating randomization procedures in experimental studies, examining potential confounding variables, or assessing the appropriateness of statistical analyses. Documentation of quality assessment procedures enhances the review's credibility and helps readers evaluate the strength of evidence presented.

Synthesis methods must be carefully selected to effectively integrate findings across multiple studies. These methods might include meta-analysis for quantitative studies, narrative synthesis for qualitative research, or mixed-methods approaches for comprehensive reviews. The chosen synthesis approach should align with the review's objectives while accommodating the diverse nature of available literature. Researchers must clearly describe their synthesis methodology, including any statistical techniques used for meta-analysis or frameworks employed for qualitative synthesis.

Critical analysis of the literature demands careful evaluation of research methodology across studies. This evaluation includes examining research design appropriateness, sampling procedures, measurement techniques, and analytical approaches. Researchers must consider how methodological choices might influence study findings and conclusions. This analysis should identify both strengths and limitations of different methodological approaches while considering their implications for result interpretation.

Reliability assessment forms another crucial aspect of critical analysis. Researchers must evaluate the consistency of findings across studies, considering factors that might contribute to divergent results. This assessment includes examining statistical reliability in quantitative studies and trustworthiness criteria in qualitative research. Particular attention should be paid to studies with conflicting findings, exploring potential methodological or contextual factors that might explain these differences.

The comparison of findings across studies requires systematic analysis of similarities and differences in results, considering both statistical significance and practical importance. Researchers should explore how differences in methodology, sample characteristics, or context might influence study outcomes. This comparative analysis helps identify patterns and trends while highlighting areas of consensus and controversy in the field.

Gap identification represents a critical outcome of literature review analysis. Researchers must systematically identify areas where current knowledge is limited or inconsistent. These gaps might include methodological limitations, unexplored populations, or theoretical uncertainties. Clear articulation of knowledge gaps helps guide future research directions while demonstrating the significance of proposed studies.

Organization of the literature review requires careful consideration of structure and flow. Thematic organization groups studies according to major concepts or research questions, allowing for clear comparison and contrast within each theme. This approach helps readers understand how different studies contribute to specific aspects of the research topic while identifying patterns across themes.

Chronological development within the review can illuminate how understanding has evolved over time. This historical perspective helps readers appreciate the progression of knowledge while identifying turning points or paradigm shifts in the field. Chronological organization might be particularly useful when discussing theoretical developments or methodological advances.

Methodological grouping allows for systematic comparison of studies using similar research approaches. This organization helps readers understand how different methodological choices might influence findings while facilitating evaluation of evidence quality across similar studies. Such grouping might be particularly useful when discussing strengths and limitations of different research approaches.

The theoretical framework provides an essential organizing principle for the literature review. Researchers should clearly articulate how different studies contribute to theoretical understanding while identifying areas where theory might need revision or expansion. This framework helps readers understand the conceptual foundations of the research while providing context for new contributions to the field.

Successful literature reviews require careful attention to all these elements while maintaining clear focus on the review's objectives. The final product should provide readers with comprehensive understanding of current knowledge while identifying promising directions for future research. Through systematic approach, critical analysis, and effective organization, literature reviews contribute significantly to the advancement of scientific knowledge in their field.

8.4 Interpreting and Discussing Results

The discussion section of scientific research represents a critical transition from objective findings to meaningful interpretations and broader implications. This section requires researchers to skillfully synthesize their results within the context of existing knowledge while acknowledging limitations and identifying future research directions.

The presentation of main findings requires a careful balance between comprehensiveness and clarity. Rather than simply restating results, researchers must distill key findings into a coherent narrative that emphasizes their significance without becoming entangled in statistical details. This summary should highlight primary outcomes while identifying meaningful patterns that emerge from the data. Unexpected findings deserve particular attention, as they often lead to new insights or research directions. The art of summarizing main findings involves selecting the most impactful results that directly address research questions while maintaining a clear connection to the study's objectives.

Pattern identification within results requires careful analysis beyond simple statistical significance. Researchers must examine relationships between different variables, temporal trends, or group differences that might suggest underlying mechanisms or broader implications. This process involves looking beyond individual data points to identify broader trends or relationships that contribute to our understanding of the phenomenon under study. Unexpected findings, while potentially challenging to interpret, often provide valuable insights and may challenge existing assumptions in the field.

Context integration represents a crucial aspect of result interpretation. Researchers must skillfully compare their findings with previous studies, identifying areas of agreement and disagreement within the existing literature. This comparison should go beyond simple agreement or disagreement to explore why differences might exist and what they might mean for our understanding of the subject matter. Theoretical implications require careful consideration of how the findings support, challenge, or extend existing theoretical frameworks in the field. This analysis might lead to modifications of existing theories or suggest the need for new theoretical approaches.

Practical applications of research findings demand thoughtful consideration of how results might influence real-world practices or policies. This requires researchers to bridge the gap between statistical significance and practical significance, considering the magnitude of effects and their relevance to actual applications. Researchers should provide specific examples of how their findings might be implemented while acknowledging any constraints or conditions that might affect practical application.

The analysis of limitations represents an essential component of honest and thorough scientific discussion. Methodology constraints must be acknowledged transparently, including any compromises made during study design or execution that might affect result interpretation. Sample limitations, such as size, composition, or selection methods, should be discussed in terms of their potential impact on findings and generalizability. This analysis should maintain a balance between acknowledging limitations and defending the study's validity.

Generalizability issues require careful consideration of the conditions under which the findings might or might not apply. This includes examining both internal and external validity, considering factors such as population characteristics, environmental conditions, or temporal aspects that might affect the broader applicability of results. Researchers should provide clear guidance about the scope of their findings' applicability while identifying factors that might influence generalizability to different contexts.

The identification of future research directions emerges naturally from a thorough discussion of findings and limitations. Research recommendations should be specific and actionable, suggesting particular areas where additional investigation could address current knowledge gaps or uncertain findings. These recommendations might include suggestions for different methodological approaches, expanded sample characteristics, or investigation of related phenomena that emerged during the study.

Methodological improvements suggested in the discussion should address specific limitations or challenges encountered during the research. These suggestions might include recommendations for enhanced measurement techniques, modified experimental designs, or alternative analytical approaches. Such recommendations contribute to the field by helping future researchers avoid similar limitations or challenges.

Points to Consider			
Main Findings Summary	**Context Integration**	**Limitations Analysis**	**Future Directions**
• Key results without statistical details	• Comparison with previous studies	• Methodology constraints	• Research recommendations
• Pattern identification	• Theoretical implications	• Sample limitations	• Methodological improvements
• Unexpected findings	• Practical applications	• Generalizability issues	• New research questions

New research questions often emerge from unexpected findings or patterns identified during the study. These questions should be clearly articulated and connected to the current findings, demonstrating how they emerge logically from the research results. Well-formulated new research questions help advance the field by identifying promising directions for future investigation.

The interpretation and discussion of results require researchers to maintain a balanced perspective, avoiding both over-interpretation and under-interpretation of findings. Claims should be supported by evidence while acknowledging uncertainty where it exists. The discussion should demonstrate scholarly judgment in weighing evidence and drawing conclusions while maintaining scientific rigor and objectivity.

Success in interpreting and discussing results ultimately depends on the researcher's ability to transform raw data into meaningful insights while maintaining scientific integrity. This process requires careful attention to detail, thorough knowledge of the field, and the ability to communicate complex findings clearly and effectively. Through thoughtful interpretation and discussion, researchers contribute not only to the specific knowledge gained from their study but also to the broader advancement of scientific understanding in their field.

8.5 Visual Presentation of Data

Visual enhancement in scientific communication plays a pivotal role in effectively conveying research findings to diverse audiences. The art of visual presentation requires careful consideration of multiple elements, each contributing to the overall clarity and impact of the scientific message.

At the foundation of visual enhancement lies several fundamental principles of visual design. Clarity stands as the cornerstone of effective scientific visualization. Researchers must prioritize the use of clear, readable fonts, particularly sans-serif varieties for digital presentations. The judicious use of white space prevents visual clutter, while a logical visual hierarchy guides viewers through the information. These elements must work in concert to ensure legibility at all intended viewing distances. Equally important is the principle of consistency throughout the presentation. This encompasses the thoughtful application of color schemes, uniform formatting for similar elements, and standardized scales across related figures. The consistent use of symbols and notation further reinforces this coherence.

Color usage demands particular attention in scientific visualization. The selection of colors must consider various factors, including accessibility for colorblind viewers and the need for effective contrast. A well-designed color palette typically contains no more than five to seven colors, carefully chosen to maintain clarity even when printed in grayscale. Colors should serve a purposeful role in conveying meaning rather than mere decoration. The consistent application of color coding across related figures helps reinforce relationships and patterns in the data.

Typography and textual elements require careful consideration in visual presentations. Font selection plays a crucial role, with professional fonts like Arial or Helvetica being standard choices. The size of text must ensure readability, with presentations typically requiring a minimum font size of 18 points. Labels and annotations demand particular attention, requiring careful placement near relevant data points while avoiding overcrowding. The inclusion of appropriate units and consistent labeling conventions enhances clarity and professionalism.

Layout and composition form another critical aspect of visual enhancement. Effective organization often employs grid-based layouts for alignment, grouping related elements while maintaining balanced visual weight. The thoughtful use of white space creates breathing room for complex information. The visual flow should guide viewers logically through the information, following consistent reading directions and clear hierarchical structures.

In the realm of data representation, enhancement strategies focus on optimizing charts and graphs for maximum clarity. This includes selecting appropriate chart types for specific data sets, removing unnecessary elements, and emphasizing data over decorative features. Scale and proportion must be carefully managed to maintain data integrity and avoid distortion of relationships. The inclusion of clear legends and scales ensures proper interpretation of the presented information.

Technical considerations play an increasingly important role in modern scientific communication. The choice between vector and raster formats, resolution requirements, and file size limitations must all be carefully weighed. Accessibility considerations have become paramount, requiring alternative text descriptions and sufficient contrast ratios to accommodate various viewing needs.

Platform-specific optimization represents another crucial aspect of visual enhancement. Print media demands high resolution (minimum 300 dpi) and careful attention to color accuracy, while digital presentations must consider screen display characteristics and varying device sizes. Each platform presents unique challenges and opportunities for effective visual communication.

The implementation of data-ink ratio optimization helps maintain focus on essential information by removing unnecessary elements such as excessive gridlines or redundant features. Visual hierarchy implementation through size variation, strategic use of white space, and consistent alignment creates clear pathways for information absorption.

Quality control measures form an essential component of visual enhancement strategies. Regular peer review of visualizations, testing for clarity and understanding, and verification of accuracy ensure the effectiveness of visual communications. Technical verification includes resolution checks, color accuracy verification, and format compatibility testing.

Special considerations arise when dealing with complex data sets. The effective use of multiple panels, clear connecting elements, and explanatory annotations helps break down complex information into digestible components. For digital formats, interactive elements must provide clear interaction cues and consistent methods, always including fallback options for static viewing.

The successful implementation of these visual enhancement strategies requires ongoing attention to detail and regular evaluation of effectiveness. The ultimate goal remains the creation of visualizations that not only accurately represent data but also effectively communicate the intended message to the target audience. Through careful application of these principles and continuous refinement of techniques, researchers can significantly enhance the impact and understanding of their scientific communications.

Effective visual presentation of data enhances understanding and engagement with research findings. The choice and execution of visual elements can significantly impact the communication of results.

Visual Enhancement Strategies

Data visualization plays a crucial role in communicating research findings effectively, with different visualization types serving distinct analytical purposes and audience needs. Understanding the appropriate application, key elements, and potential pitfalls of each visualization type enables researchers to present their data with maximum impact and clarity.

Data Visualization Guidelines				
Visual Type	**Best Used For**	**Key Elements**	**Common Pitfalls**	**Design Tips**
Line Graphs	• Trends over time • Continuous relationships • Multiple series comparison	• Clear axes • Legend • Proper scaling	• Too many lines • Unclear intersections • Missing labels	• Use distinct colors • Include error bars • Clear line weights
Bar Charts	• Category comparisons • Frequency distributions • Grouped data	• Consistent spacing • Clear labels • Error bars	• 3D effects • Truncated axes • Unclear scales	• Use consistent colors • Start at zero • Appropriate width
Scatter Plots	• Correlation analysis • Distribution patterns • Clustering	• Axis scales • Data points • Trend lines	• Overplotting • Missing units • Poor scaling	• Use transparency • Include R^2 values • Clear markers
Box Plots	• Data distribution • Outlier identification • Group comparisons	• Quartiles • Whiskers • Outliers	• Unclear statistics • Missing legends • Poor spacing	• Show all data points • Label outliers • Consistent width
Heat Maps	• Multi-variable patterns • Spatial distribution • Large datasets	• Color scale • Grid layout • Legend	• Poor color choice • Unclear scaling • Missing values	• Use colorblind-friendly palettes • Include scale bars • Clear boundaries

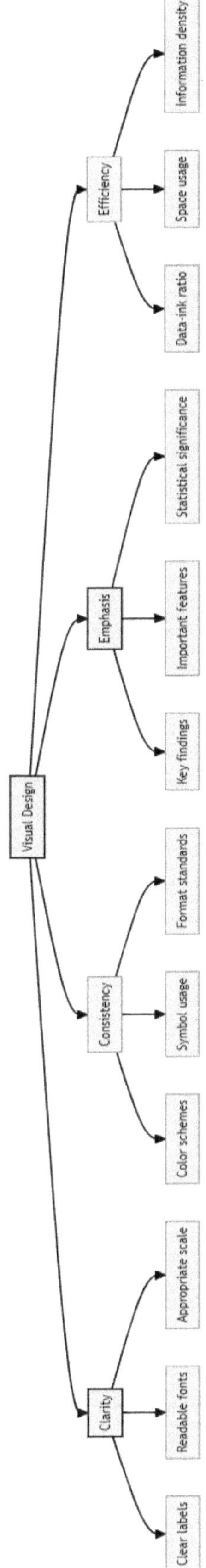

Fig. 8.3. Principles of Visual Design in Scientific Communication

Line graphs excel in displaying temporal trends and continuous relationships, making them ideal for longitudinal studies and multiple series comparisons. Essential elements include clearly labeled axes, comprehensive legends, and appropriate scaling. While line graphs effectively communicate trends, researchers must avoid common pitfalls such as overcrowding with too many lines or unclear intersections. Design best practices include utilizing distinct colors for different series, incorporating error bars where appropriate, and maintaining clear line weights to ensure readability.

Bar charts and **scatter plots** serve complementary purposes in data presentation. Bar charts effectively communicate categorical comparisons and frequency distributions, requiring consistent spacing and clear labeling. Key considerations include avoiding deceptive 3D effects and truncated axes. Scatter plots, particularly valuable for correlation analysis and distribution patterns, require careful attention to axis scaling and trend line representation. The inclusion of R^2 values and appropriate marker sizes enhances their interpretative value.

Box plots and **heat maps** represent more specialized visualization tools. Box plots excel in displaying data distributions and outlier identification, requiring clear representation of quartiles, whiskers, and outliers. Effective box plots maintain consistent width and clearly label statistical elements. Heat maps, optimal for multi-variable patterns and large datasets, demand careful color selection and clear scaling. Success with heat maps relies heavily on colorblind-friendly palettes and clear boundary definitions.

Across all visualization types, common principles emerge: maintain clarity through appropriate labeling, avoid decorative elements that obscure data, and ensure accessibility through thoughtful color choices and scaling. Each visualization type should be selected based on the specific data characteristics and intended message, with careful attention to both technical accuracy and visual appeal. This balanced approach ensures that visualizations effectively communicate complex data while maintaining scientific rigor.

8.6 Publishing and Presenting Research

The journey from completed research to publication requires careful attention to both content and process.

8.6.1 Journal Submission Process

The journey from completed research to published scientific article follows a structured yet complex path that requires careful attention to detail and adherence to established protocols. Understanding this process is crucial for researchers seeking to disseminate their findings effectively through peer-reviewed journals.

The journal submission process begins with the critical step of manuscript preparation. This initial phase requires researchers to transform their research findings into a coherent narrative that adheres to scientific writing conventions. The manuscript must be structured according to standard scientific format, including abstract, introduction, methods, results, discussion, and references. Each section demands meticulous attention to detail, with careful consideration given to clarity, accuracy, and completeness of information presented.

Journal selection represents a crucial decision point in the submission process. Researchers must carefully evaluate potential journals based on several criteria, including scope alignment, impact factor, target audience, and publication timeframes. Additionally, practical considerations such as publication fees, open access options, and journal reputation play significant roles in this decision. It's advisable to review recent issues of potential target journals to ensure your research aligns with their publishing patterns and interests.

The preparation of submission materials extends beyond the main manuscript. Most journals require a compelling cover letter that introduces the research and argues for its significance and appropriateness for the journal. This document serves as the researchers' opportunity to make a strong first impression on the editorial team. Additionally, many journals require specific supplementary materials, such as data availability statements, funding declarations, and conflict of interest disclosures.

Initial submission typically occurs through an online submission system specific to each journal or publishing group. This process involves uploading the manuscript and all supporting documents in the required formats, often including separate files for figures, tables, and supplementary materials. The submission system usually requires detailed information about authors, including their affiliations, contact information, and contributions to the work. Many journals also request suggestions for potential reviewers, though the final selection remains at the editors' discretion.

The editorial review represents the first major hurdle in the publication process. Upon submission, the manuscript undergoes an initial screening by the editorial team to ensure it meets basic requirements and falls within the journal's scope. This phase may result in immediate rejection if the manuscript fails to meet essential criteria or is deemed inappropriate for the journal's readership. Successfully passing this initial screen leads to the assignment of an handling editor who oversees the peer review process.

Peer review stands as the cornerstone of scientific publishing, serving as a critical quality control mechanism. During this phase, the manuscript is typically sent to two to four expert reviewers in the field. These reviewers evaluate the work's scientific merit, methodology, presentation, and significance. The review process can take anywhere from a few weeks to several months, depending on the journal and reviewer availability. Reviewers provide detailed feedback and recommendations to the editor regarding the manuscript's suitability for publication.

Following peer review, authors receive a decision letter along with reviewer comments. The possible decisions typically include acceptance (rare for initial submissions), minor revision, major revision, or rejection. In the case of revisions, authors must carefully address each reviewer comment and prepare a detailed response document outlining the changes made to the manuscript. This response should be thorough and professional, addressing all concerns raised while maintaining a constructive dialogue with reviewers and editors.

The revision process often involves substantial changes to the manuscript, potentially including additional experiments, analyses, or major rewrites of sections. Authors must typically complete these revisions within a specified timeframe, though extensions can often be requested if necessary. The revised manuscript and response to reviewers undergo another round of evaluation, either by the original reviewers or sometimes by new reviewers.

Upon acceptance, the manuscript enters the production phase. This stage involves various technical checks, including format compliance, figure quality verification, and reference accuracy. Authors must carefully review proofs provided by the publisher, checking for any errors introduced during the typesetting process. This represents the final opportunity to make minor corrections before publication.

The final steps in the publication process involve administrative tasks such as signing copyright transfer agreements or open access licenses, paying any applicable publication fees, and providing final versions of figures in high-resolution formats. Many journals also now require data availability statements and the deposit of raw data in appropriate repositories.

Post-publication activities have become increasingly important in the modern scientific landscape. Authors are often encouraged to promote their published work through various channels, including social media, institutional websites, and academic networks. Many journals provide metrics on article views, downloads, and citations, helping authors track their work's impact in the scientific community.

Throughout the submission process, professional communication remains essential. Authors should maintain courteous and timely correspondence with editors and reviewers, adhering to deadlines and journal policies. When challenges arise, such as delays in revision submission or disagreements with reviewer comments, these should be handled professionally through appropriate channels.

Understanding and effectively navigating the journal submission process significantly increases the likelihood of successful publication. While the process can be lengthy and sometimes frustrating, it serves the crucial function of ensuring the quality and reliability of published scientific literature. Success in publishing often comes from careful preparation, attention to detail, and persistence through the various stages of the submission and review process.

8.6.2 Conference Presentation

Conference presentations represent a vital platform for sharing research findings with the scientific community, fostering collaboration, and receiving immediate feedback from peers. Whether delivered as oral presentations, poster sessions, or workshop formats, effective conference communication requires careful preparation and attention to both content and delivery.

The art of conference presentation begins with understanding the distinct presentation formats and their specific requirements. Oral presentations typically allow researchers 10-20 minutes to present their work, followed by a brief question-and-answer session. These time constraints necessitate careful selection of content, focusing on key findings while maintaining sufficient context for audience understanding. The presentation structure must flow logically, typically beginning with a brief introduction that captures attention and establishes relevance, followed by concise methods, clear results, and impactful conclusions.

Poster presentations, while different in format from oral presentations, demand equal attention to detail and organization. The visual layout of a scientific poster must guide viewers through the research story efficiently, as viewers often have limited time to engage with each poster. The design should employ a clear visual hierarchy, with the most important information prominently displayed and supporting details readily accessible. Successful poster presentations also require researchers to prepare an effective "elevator pitch" - a brief, engaging overview that can be delivered in 2-3 minutes to interested viewers.

Visual elements play a crucial role in both presentation formats. For oral presentations, slides should enhance rather than duplicate the spoken message. Each slide should convey a single main point, using clear, high-quality graphics and minimal text. The recommended guideline of no more than 6-7 lines of text per slide helps maintain audience engagement and prevents information overload. For posters, the challenge lies in balancing comprehensive information with visual appeal, using white space effectively to prevent overcrowding and enhance readability.

The delivery of oral presentations requires careful attention to verbal and non-verbal communication elements. Speech pace should be measured and deliberate, with strategic pauses to emphasize key points and allow audience comprehension. Eye contact with audience members helps maintain engagement and gauge understanding. Body language should project confidence and enthusiasm while remaining professional. Practice sessions before the actual presentation are invaluable for refining timing, identifying potential stumbling points, and building confidence.

Engagement with the audience differentiates conference presentations from other forms of scientific communication. During oral presentations, speakers must remain attuned to audience reactions and be prepared to adjust their delivery accordingly. The question-and-answer session requires careful listening and thoughtful, concise responses. For poster presentations, presenters must be prepared to engage in detailed discussions with interested viewers while remaining aware of others waiting to view the poster.

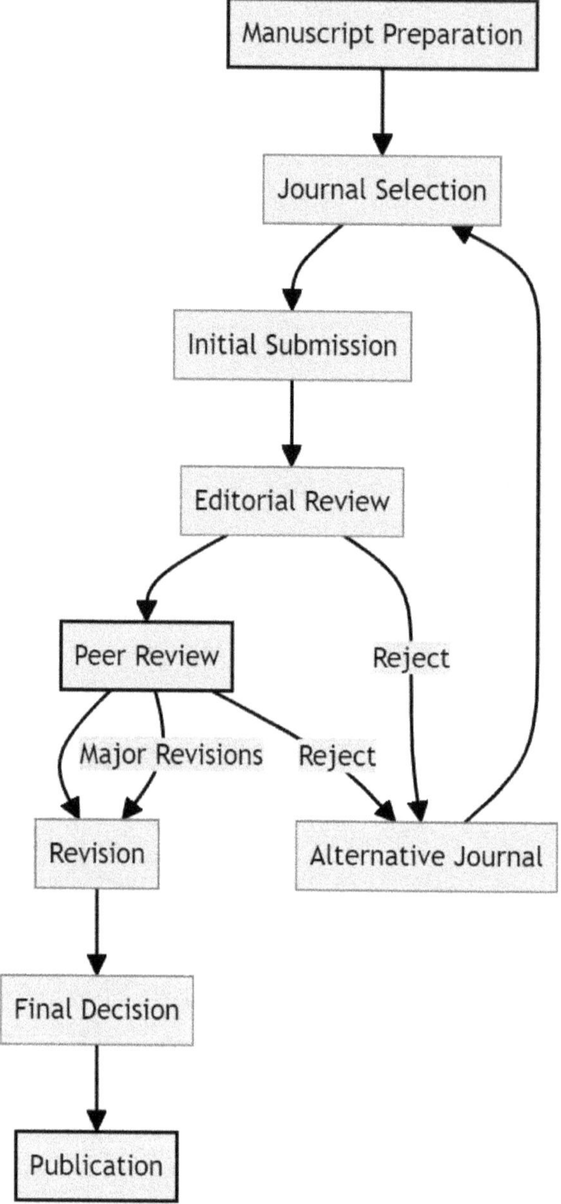

Fig. 8.4. Research Publication Process

Technical considerations require careful attention during preparation. Oral presentation slides should be tested on different devices to ensure compatibility and readability. Backup copies of presentations should be available in multiple formats and storage devices. For poster presentations, printing quality and transportation logistics must be considered well in advance. Many conferences now also offer virtual or hybrid presentation options, requiring familiarity with relevant platforms and potential technical challenges.

Time management represents a critical skill in conference presentations. For oral presentations, speakers must rehearse thoroughly to ensure they can complete their presentation within the allotted time while maintaining a natural delivery pace. This often requires difficult decisions about content inclusion and level of detail. Poster presenters must manage their time effectively during poster sessions, balancing detailed discussions with individual viewers against the need to engage with multiple audience members.

The handling of questions requires specific preparation and skills. Presenters should anticipate potential questions and prepare clear, concise responses. When faced with unexpected questions, it's important to maintain professionalism while acknowledging limitations in knowledge or data. The ability to turn challenging questions into opportunities for meaningful discussion demonstrates scholarly maturity and can lead to valuable research insights or collaborations.

Professional networking opportunities during conferences should not be overlooked. Effective presenters use their presentations as springboards for establishing connections with colleagues in their field. This might involve following up with interested audience members, exchanging contact information, or discussing potential collaborations. The presentation itself often serves as an introduction to more detailed discussions during conference social events or break periods.

Feedback collection and incorporation represent important aspects of conference presentations. Presenters should be open to constructive criticism and suggestions from audience members, noting potential improvements for future presentations or research directions. Many conferences provide formal feedback mechanisms, and presenters should actively seek such input to enhance their presentation skills and research development.

Conference Presentation Guidelines				
Presentation Type	**Key Elements**	**Time Management**	**Visual Elements**	**Delivery Tips**
Oral Presentation	• Clear structure • Key messages • Engaging delivery	• Practice timing • Q&A allocation • Smooth transitions	• Limited text • Clear figures • Consistent design	• Eye contact • Clear speech • Professional stance
Poster Presentation	• Visual hierarchy • Logical flow • Key findings	• Brief overview • Interactive discussion • Time management	• Large fonts • Clear graphics • White space	• Elevator pitch • Active engagement • Physical positioning
Flash Talk	• Core message • Essential data • Impact statement	• Strict timing • Focused content • Clear conclusion	• Minimal slides • Key visuals • Clear transitions	• Dynamic delivery • Pace control • Strong conclusion
Workshop	• Interactive elements • Practical examples • Clear objectives	• Section planning • Activity timing • Discussion periods	• Handouts • Demonstrations • Visual aids	• Audience engagement • Clear instructions • Flexibility

Conference presentations also provide valuable opportunities for young researchers to develop their professional identity within their field. Through these presentations, they learn to articulate their research clearly, defend their methods and conclusions, and engage in scholarly discourse with peers and senior researchers. The experience gained through conference presentations contributes significantly to professional development and career advancement in scientific research.

The ability to effectively present research at conferences represents a crucial skill in scientific careers. Success requires careful preparation, practice, and attention to both content and delivery. Through thoughtful consideration of these elements and continuous refinement of presentation skills, researchers can maximize the impact of their conference presentations and advance their professional development in the scientific community.

8.6.3 Publishing Success Strategies

The path to successful publication in scientific journals requires careful attention to multiple stages of the publication process. Understanding and implementing effective strategies at each stage significantly increases the likelihood of publication success and helps maintain the quality of scientific literature.

Pre-submission strategies form the foundation of successful publication efforts. Journal scope alignment represents the first critical consideration. Researchers must thoroughly evaluate potential journals by reviewing their aims and scope statements, examining recently published articles, and assessing the journal's target audience. This evaluation should extend beyond simple topic matching to consider the methodological approaches, theoretical frameworks, and level of sophistication typically featured in the journal. Additionally, researchers should consider practical factors such as the journal's impact factor, publication timeline, and acceptance rates.

Format requirements demand meticulous attention during the pre-submission phase. Each journal maintains specific formatting guidelines covering aspects such as manuscript structure, word limits, reference styles, and figure specifications. Careful adherence to these requirements demonstrates professionalism and prevents unnecessary delays in the review process. Authors should create a detailed checklist of formatting requirements and systematically verify compliance before submission. This attention to detail extends to file naming conventions, figure resolution requirements, and supplementary material formats.

The preparation of an effective cover letter represents another crucial pre-submission task. A well-crafted cover letter serves as the author's opportunity to make a compelling case for their manuscript's publication. It should clearly articulate the research's significance, originality, and relevance to the journal's readership. The cover letter should also address any potential concerns about the manuscript, such as overlap with previously published work or ethical considerations. Many successful authors use the cover letter to suggest potential reviewers while also identifying any individuals who might have conflicts of interest.

Author guidelines compliance extends beyond basic formatting to encompass ethical requirements, data availability statements, funding declarations, and conflict of interest disclosures. Authors must carefully review and comply with all journal policies regarding authorship criteria, ethical approval documentation, and data sharing requirements. This comprehensive compliance helps prevent delays and demonstrates professional rigor in the submission process.

During the review phase, success strategies focus on effective interaction with editors and reviewers. Prompt responses to reviewer comments and editorial decisions demonstrate professionalism and maintain momentum in the publication process. Authors should carefully track review deadlines and request extensions if needed, rather than allowing deadlines to lapse without communication.

The systematic addressing of reviewer comments represents a critical skill in the publication process. Successful authors create detailed response documents that address each reviewer comment point by point. This response should clearly indicate the changes made to the manuscript, providing page and line numbers for easy reference. Where authors disagree with reviewer suggestions, they should provide clear, evidence-based justifications for their position while maintaining a respectful and professional tone.

Professional communication throughout the review process significantly influences publication success. Authors should maintain courteous and constructive dialogue with editors and reviewers, even when facing critical comments or disagreements. This professional approach helps build positive relationships within the scientific community and can influence future publication efforts.

Post-acceptance strategies ensure the final published article meets high-quality standards and achieves maximum impact. Proof checking requires careful attention to detail, as this represents the final opportunity to correct errors before publication. Authors should review proofs thoroughly, checking for accuracy in text, figures, tables, and references. Special attention should be paid to mathematical equations, special characters, and complex formatting elements that might be affected during typesetting.

Publishing Success Strategies in Scientific Research		
STAGES		
Pre-submission	**During Review**	**Post-acceptance**
• Journal scope alignment	• Prompt responses	• Proof checking
• Format requirements	• Systematic addressing of comments	• Figure quality
• Cover letter preparation	• Clear response document	• Copyright forms
• Author guidelines compliance	• Professional communication	• Publication promotion

Figure quality verification becomes particularly important during the production phase. Authors must ensure that all figures meet the journal's technical requirements for resolution, size, and format. This often involves preparing different versions of figures for online and print publication, considering color requirements, and ensuring clarity at different scales.

Copyright and licensing requirements must be addressed promptly upon acceptance. Authors should carefully review copyright transfer agreements or open access licenses, ensuring all authors understand and agree to the terms. Many journals now offer various licensing options, and authors must make informed decisions about copyright retention and sharing rights.

Publication promotion strategies have become increasingly important in the modern scientific landscape. Authors should develop a comprehensive plan for promoting their published work through various channels, including social media, institutional websites, and academic networks. Many journals provide tools and resources for article promotion, and authors should take advantage of these opportunities to increase their work's visibility and impact.

Success in scientific publishing requires careful attention to these various strategies throughout the publication process. Authors who systematically implement these approaches while maintaining professional standards and attention to detail significantly increase their chances of successful publication and broader impact of their research in the scientific community.

8.6.4 Structuring Scientific Presentations

Scientific presentations require careful organization and timing to effectively communicate research findings within allocated time constraints. Understanding how to structure content across different time segments ensures comprehensive coverage while maintaining audience engagement and meeting session requirements.

The opening segment, typically allocated 2-3 minutes, serves as the critical foundation for the entire presentation. This period must immediately capture audience attention through a compelling hook statement. Effective hooks might include a striking statistic, a thought-provoking question, or a relevant real-world problem that contextualizes the research. Following the hook, presenters must efficiently establish the research context, situating their work within the broader scientific landscape. This contextualization should avoid excessive background detail while providing sufficient information for audience understanding. The opening segment concludes with a clear statement of research objectives, typically presented as specific aims or research questions. These objectives should be concise, measurable, and directly related to the subsequent presentation content.

The methods section, allocated 3-4 minutes, requires careful selection of essential methodological information. Rather than detailed protocols, this segment should provide a clear overview of the study design that enables audience understanding of the research approach. Key methodologies should be highlighted, focusing on novel or particularly significant aspects of the research process. The analysis approach should be presented efficiently, emphasizing statistical methods or analytical frameworks that directly support the main findings. Visual aids during this segment might include flow charts, experimental design diagrams, or simplified methodology schematics that help audience comprehension without overwhelming them with detail.

The results section, typically the longest segment at 5-6 minutes, demands careful organization and clear presentation of findings. Key findings should be presented in a logical sequence, with each result building upon previous ones to create a coherent narrative. Supporting data must be carefully selected to provide evidence for main conclusions while avoiding information overload. Visual presentations play a crucial role in this segment, requiring clear, well-designed figures that effectively communicate complex data. Graphs, charts, and images should be carefully explained but not over-explained, allowing the visual elements to support and enhance the verbal presentation.

The conclusion segment, allocated 2-3 minutes, must effectively synthesize the presentation's key messages. Main implications of the research should be clearly articulated, emphasizing the significance of the findings for both theoretical understanding and practical applications. Future directions should be briefly outlined, indicating potential research paths that emerge from the current findings. The take-home message should provide a memorable conclusion that reinforces the presentation's main contribution to the field.

Timing considerations extend beyond simple segment allocation. Transitions between segments must be smooth and efficient, typically accomplished through clear verbal cues or transitional slides. Each segment should be practiced to ensure precise timing while maintaining a natural delivery pace. Presenters should plan for slight timing variations, identifying content that could be abbreviated or expanded as needed without compromising the presentation's core message.

Visual elements require careful consideration within the time-based framework. Slides should be designed to support rather than duplicate the verbal presentation, with each visual element timed to appear at appropriate moments. The number of slides should be carefully calculated to allow adequate time for explanation while maintaining presentation flow. A general guideline suggests one slide per minute, though this may vary depending on content complexity and presentation style.

Question-and-answer preparation must be integrated into the timing strategy. While the main presentation fits within the allocated time frame, presenters should prepare concise responses to anticipated questions. This preparation helps maintain overall session timing while ensuring thorough engagement with audience inquiries.

Practice sessions play a crucial role in refining the time-based presentation structure. Multiple run-throughs help identify segments that consistently run long or short, allowing for adjustment before the actual presentation. Recording practice sessions can provide valuable feedback on timing, pace, and transition effectiveness.

Technical considerations must also be integrated into the timing strategy. Presenters should plan for potential technical delays or issues, having backup plans that can be implemented without disrupting the presentation's timing. File access, slide transitions, and any special features should be tested in advance to ensure smooth execution within the time constraints.

Scientific Presentation Template			
Opening (2-3 minutes)	**Methods (3-4 minutes)**	**Results (5-6 minutes)**	**Conclusion (2-3 minutes)**
• Hook statement	• Study design overview	• Key findings	• Main implications
• Research context	• Key methodologies	• Supporting data	• Future directions
• Clear objectives	• Analysis approach	• Visual presentations	• Take-home message

The success of a scientific presentation often depends on this careful balance of content and timing. A well-structured presentation that adheres to these time allocations while maintaining clear communication of research findings demonstrates professional competence and respect for audience time. Through careful preparation and practice, presenters can effectively convey their research within these time constraints while maintaining audience engagement and understanding.

Glossary

Discovery consists of seeing what everybody has seen and thinking what nobody has thought.

- Albert Szent-Györgyi

Accidental Sampling	A sampling method based on convenience in accessing the population, where any available person can be contacted until reaching the required sample size.
Action Research	A systematic research approach that combines community involvement with cyclical processes of planning, action, observation, and reflection, aimed at solving practical problems while generating new knowledge. It emphasizes active participation of community members in all research phases from problem identification to implementation of solutions.
Active Variable	A variable in research that can be deliberately changed, controlled, or manipulated by the researcher to study its effects on other variables in the study. Used in causality studies.
After-only Design	Research design where baseline information is constructed from respondents' recall or existing records after an intervention.
Alternate Hypothesis	A statement explicitly specifying the relationship considered true if the research hypothesis proves wrong. Represented as H_1 or H_A.
Ambiguous Question	A question containing multiple meanings that can be interpreted differently by respondents.
Applied Research	Research where techniques, procedures, and methods are applied to collect information about various aspects of a situation for purposes such as policy formulation, program development, and evaluation.
Area Chart	Graphical representation showing information about subcategories with shaded areas under curves.
Attitudinal Scales	Measurement tools designed to measure attitudes, including Likert, Thurstone, and Guttman scales.
Bar Chart	Graphical display of categorical data using spaced rectangles.
Before-and-after Studies	Design comparing two sets of cross-sectional data to measure change over time.
Bias	A deliberate attempt to either conceal or highlight something found in research, or deliberately using an inappropriate procedure to obtain desired information due to vested interest.

Blind Studies — Studies or research where the study population doesn't know whether they're receiving real or fake treatment, designed to isolate the placebo effect.

Case Study — A research design based on the assumption that a single case can provide insight into similar cases. It involves thorough, holistic, in-depth exploration of selected aspects.

Categorical Variables — Variables measured in categories rather than continuous values.

Chance Variable — Variables affecting responses randomly without systematic patterns.

Closed Question — Questions with predetermined possible answers.

Cluster Sampling — Sampling technique dividing population into groups based on visible characteristics.

Cohort Studies — Research based on studying groups with common characteristics (e.g., birth year, graduation year) over time.

Collaborative Enquiry — Research advocating close collaboration between researcher and participants.

Content Analysis — A method of analyzing qualitative data by examining interview contents or observational notes to identify emerging main themes.

Control Group — In experimental studies, the group not exposed to the experimental intervention, used to measure impact of extraneous variables.

Correlational Studies — Research investigating relationships between variables.

Dependent Variable — The variable that changes as a result of the independent variable's influence in causality studies.

Descriptive Studies — Research focusing on systematic description rather than relationship examination.

Experimental Studies — Research where the researcher introduces an intervention and observes its effects over time.

Extraneous Variables — Variables other than the independent variable that can affect the relationship between independent and dependent variables.

Face Validity — Initial form of validity checking whether a measure appears to measure what it claims.

Feasibility Study — Preliminary study investigating possibility of larger-scale research.

Focus Group — Qualitative research strategy using facilitated group discussions.

Holistic Research — Philosophy examining phenomena from multiple perspectives.

Hypothesis — An assumption, suspicion, or idea about a phenomenon or relationship that becomes the basis for inquiry and investigation.

Independent Variable — The variable responsible for bringing about change in a phenomenon in causality studies or in experimental studies.

In-depth Interviewing — Detailed interview method with complete content and structure freedom.

Indicators — Measurable elements reflecting broader concepts.

Informed Consent — Participants' agreement to participate after full disclosure of study details.

Interval — Equal intervals between points

Interview Schedule — A written list of questions used by an interviewer in person-to-person interactions.

Likert Scale — Attitude measurement scale using equal-weighted statements.

Longitudinal Study — Research collecting data from same subjects over extended time periods.

Matching — Technique forming comparable groups in experimental studies.

Mixed Methods — Research approaches combining both qualitative and quantitative methods to provide comprehensive understanding.

Nominal — Basic categorization, without order.

Non-experimental Studies — Research examining existing phenomena without manipulation.

Non-probability Sampling — Sampling not following probability theory.

Observation — Systematic way of watching and recording behavior or phenomena.

Operational Definition — Specific, measurable definition of research concepts.

Ordinal — Ordered or Ranked categories.

Panel Studies — Prospective studies collecting information from same respondents over time.

Participatory Research — Research actively involving study participants in the research process.

Population — Complete group being studied.

Primary Data — Data collected directly through interviews, surveys, observations, experiments, etc.

Qualitative Research — Research based on empiricism, following an unstructured, flexible approach focusing on in-depth understanding and small samples. Research rooted in rationalism, following structured methodology, emphasizing larger samples and quantifiable variations.

Quantitative Research — Structured approach emphasizing numerical data and statistical analysis.

Questionnaire — Written list of research questions for respondents to answer.

Random Sampling — Selection giving each population element equal chance of selection.

Ratio — True zero point plus all other scale properties.

Reliability

The ability of a research instrument to provide similar results when used repeatedly under similar conditions.

Research Design

A procedural plan adopted to answer questions validly, objectively, accurately, and economically.

Sampling

The process of selecting respondents from a larger population to collect information.

Scale

Method of measurement classifying respondents.

Secondary Data

Existing data used for research purposes.

Secondary

Using existing data from previous research, documents, records or using existing data sources.

Statistical Analysis

Mathematical methods for analyzing numerical data.

Study Population

The complete group about whom information is desired (denoted by N).

Theoretical Framework

Network of theories relevant to research topic.

Triangulation

Using multiple methods or data sources to enhance study validity.

Validity

Accuracy and appropriateness of research methods and measurements, or the appropriateness of research steps and an instrument's ability to measure what it's designed to measure.

Variables

Concepts, images, or perceptions capable of measurement and taking different values.

Index